University of York Studies in Economics

GENERAL EDITORS

Professor A. T. Peacock
Department of Economics

Professor J. Wiseman
Institute of Social and Economic Research

6

A THEORY OF ECONOMIC INTEGRATION FOR DEVELOPING COUNTRIES

University of York Studies in Economics

A THEORY OF
ECONOMIC INTEGRATION
FOR DEVELOPING
COUNTRIES

ILLUSTRATED BY CARIBBEAN COUNTRIES

Fuat Andic
Suphan Andic
Douglas Dosser

London
GEORGE ALLEN AND UNWIN LTD

First published in 1971

ISBN 0 04 330095 2

Printed in Great Britain in 11 pt Times Roman
by Alden & Mowbray Ltd at the Alden Press, Oxford

ACKNOWLEDGMENTS

This study was prepared under the auspices of the Institute of Caribbean Studies of the University of Puerto Rico with funds provided by the Ford Foundation. We would like to express our sincerest thanks to the staff members of the Secretariats of CARIFTA, CACM, EEC, and LAFTA for providing us with extremely useful material, published and unpublished, and for giving us very generously their time to answer our questions and queries. Facilities provided by the Universities of York and Puerto Rico were of great assistance. The Caribbean Regional Library and Institute of Social & Economic Research at York rendered their services to us in their customary spirit of co-operation and courtesy. Last but not least we would like to express our appreciation to our research assistants, R. Funkhouser, T. Hitiris, C. Egurbida, J. Barreto, R. Cao and D. Gandia, who carried the great burden of work cheerfully and with great dedication.

NOTE ON THE AUTHORS

Fuat Andic is Professor of Economics at the University of Puerto Rico and has worked as a consultant to the United Nations and to various governments in Central America and the Caribbean. Among his publications are *The Caribbean in Transition* and *Government Finance and Planned Development*.

Suphan Andic is Associate Professor of Economics at the University of Puerto Rico. She is co-author of two works, *A Fiscal Survey of the French Caribbean* and *Government Finance and Planned Development*.

Douglas Dosser is Professor of Economic Theory at the University of York. He is co-author of *Fiscal Harmonization in Common Markets, Studies in Trade Liberalization* and *The Economy of Liberia*, and author of *Taxes in the EEC and Britain: The Problem of Harmonization*.

CONTENTS

GLOSSARY OF ABBREVIATIONS

ALALC Asociación Latinoamericana de Libre Comercio (see LAFTA)
CABEI Central American Bank for Economic Integration
CACM Central American Common Market
CARIFTA Caribbean Free Trade Association
CEPAL Comisión Económica para América Latina (see ECLA)
ECCM Eastern Caribbean Common Market
ECLA Economic Commission for Latin America
EDF European Development Fund
EEC European Economic Community
EFTA European Free Trade Association
EIB European Investment Bank
ICAITI Instituto Centroamericano de Investigación y Tecnología Industrial (Central American Institute of Industrial Research and Technology)
IDB Interamerican Development Bank
INTAL Instituto para la Integración de América Latina (Institute of Latin American Integration)
IMF International Monetary Fund
LAFTA Latin American Free Trade Association
MCCA Mercado Comun Centroamericano (see CACM)
OAS Organisation of American States
RDB Regional Development Bank for the Caribbean; also known as CARIBANK
SIECA Secretaría Permanente del Tratado General de Integración Económica Centroamericana (Permanent Secretariat of the General Treaty of Central American Economic Integration)
SITC Standard Industrial Trade Classification

Part I

A THEORY OF ECONOMIC INTEGRATION FOR DEVELOPING COUNTRIES

Chapter 1

QUALITATIVE ASPECTS OF THE THEORY

It is customary to distinguish three stages of economic integration. The first is the establishment of some form of customs union or free trade area. The second involves tax union, i.e. tax harmonization measures added to action on tariffs. The third stage is the formation of a common market, which essentially adds unimpeded factor flows to the previous two stages. The theory of these three stages of integration is fairly well developed for mature economies, although not entirely so. But our main interest lies in developing economies. Confining ourselves to the first stage, we shall endeavour to modify and extend the theory for mature economies so that it is more appropriate to the situation in which developing countries find themselves.

In evaluating the effects of the establishment of a customs union or free trade area, there are two different categories into which work may be divided. It is not quite correct to distinguish these between the theoretical and the statistical. Rather, the first category is entirely non-quantitative and attempts to state whether a particular movement towards integration is economically desirable or not according to general reasoning about the economies concerned; this is simply a qualitative economic analysis, resulting in a number of non-quantitative propositions. The second approach is statistical, and attempts to quantify the gains in trade, national income or welfare from a particular quantitatively specified movement toward integration. We shall maintain this distinction and devote the present chapter to the qualitative aspects.

Most of this qualitative analysis has been conducted in terms

13

of *trade creation* and *trade diversion*. The initial situation is simply the existence of tariffs, and the assumed changes are their complete removal. The resulting *trade creation* and *trade diversion* is mainly deduced from the types of products which the members of the union were producing in the initial situation. *Trade creation* occurs if, prior to the formation of the customs union, potential union countries were producing a commodity behind tariff walls where, after formation of the union, one of the union partners becomes the complete supplier for the union. Since production is relocated in the least-cost location within the union, *trade creation* has a beneficial effect on the national income of the union and of the world. *Trade diversion* occurs if one of the member countries was producing the commodity before formation of the customs union inefficiently (as a high cost producer) due to its protection behind a tariff wall; on the formation of the union this country now captures the whole of the union market. This is certainly a loss in world national income, due to the deterioration in specialization on a world scale, but it may be a loss or a gain to the total national income of the union.

The most celebrated conclusion from this simple analysis is that the formation of a customs union will be most beneficial where trade creation dominates, and that this occurs when the constituent economies are competitive in products, rather than complementary, prior to the formation of a customs union.

This analysis from Viner has been extended by Meade and Lipsey,[1] adding so-called consumption effects to the above production effects. These refinements, which we shall not go into, lead to further qualitative propositions, a long list from Meade, and the following two from Lipsey: (i) a customs union is more likely to raise welfare the higher the proportion of trade with the country's union partner and the lower the proportion with the outside world; (ii) a customs union is more likely to

[1] J. Viner, *The Customs Union Issue*, Carnegie Endowment for International Peace, New York, 1950. J. E. Meade, *The Theory of Customs Unions*, North Holland, Amsterdam, 1955. R. G. Lipsey, 'The Theory of Customs Unions: Trade Diversion and Welfare', *Economica*, New Series, 24, February 1957. *Idem*, 'The Theory of Customs Unions: A General Survey', *Economic Journal*, 70, September 1960.

raise welfare the lower the total volume of foreign trade is relative to domestic purchases prior to the formation of the union.

Enough has been said to demonstrate a major proposition about conventional customs union theory and developing countries. It is that if we confine ourselves to conventional customs union theory we are bound to conclude that customs unions between developing countries are not beneficial. The Vinerian conclusion implies that *trade diversion* will greatly exceed *trade creation*, because it is usually manufacturing countries which are competitive and developing countries which are complementary both to manufacturing countries and to each other. And Brown[2] has pointed out that the opposite of the Lipsey conditions usually holds for less-developed countries' trade—they trade with developed countries rather than each other, and they often have very large foreign trade sectors in relation to national output.

In the face of this situation some economists, like Allen, Meier, and Mikesell[3] have repudiated the standard customs union theory as being relevant to developing countries. Others have taken a different course: not to repudiate customs union theory as completely irrelevant to developing countries, but to reject that brand of it which is current as applicable only to developed economies, and to realize that there may be forms of customs union, and criteria of judging their success other than the conventional ones, which may be of value in the analysis and policy of less-developed countries. This new way of thinking on customs unions has been developed by Mikesell in a second paper, by Bhambri, Kitamura, Urquidi, Linder and by Cooper and Massell.[4]

[2] A. J. Brown, 'Customs Union vs. Economic Separatism in Developing Countries', I and II, *Yorkshire Bulletin*, May 1961.

[3] R. L. Allen, 'Integration in Less Developed Areas', *Kyklos*, 14, 315–34, fasc. 3, 1961. G. M. Meier, 'Effects of a Customs Union on Economic Development', *Social and Economic Studies*, March 1960. R. F. Mikesell, 'The Movement Toward Regional Trading Groups in Latin America', in *Latin American Issues: Essays and Comments*, ed. A. O. Hirschman, The Twentieth Century Fund, New York, 1961.

[4] R. F. Mikesell, 'The Theory of Common Markets as Applied to Regional Arrangements Among Developing Countries', in *International Trade Theory*

There are two strands of thought running through this list of writers on a new customs union theory for developing countries: the first strand concerns industrialization and the second, the saving of scarce foreign exchange by import substitution. These are both, of course, common elements in the theory of development. By drawing them out of development theory and integrating them with customs union theory it is quickly evident that the conventional evaluation criteria of conventional customs union theory are insufficient because they do not give weight to either of these two factors. Thus customs union may score rather badly looking at trade alone, with a predominance of *trade diversion*, but this may be consistent with promoting much-desired industrialization in the less-developed countries involved. Again, *trade diversion* means import substitution and also permanent savings of scarce foreign exchange which promote development.

In general the industrialization aspect of customs unions has been emphasized by Urquidi, some of the many interesting writings on the East African market,[5] and most of all by Cooper and Massell. The aspect of import substitution to save foreign exchange has been emphasized by Bhambri, Kitamura, Mikesell's second paper, the ECLA report and by Staffan Linder. In our own contribution we will take the Cooper and Massell paper as the prime building block on the industrialization side, and the analysis by Linder for the foreign exchange side.

in a Developing World, ed. R. F. Harrod and D. C. Hague, Macmillan, London, 1963. R. S. Bhambri, 'Customs Unions and Under-Developed Countries', *Economica Internazionale*, XV, May 1962. H. Kitamura, 'Economic Theory and Regional Economic Integration of Asia', in *Latin American Economic Integration*, ed. M. S. Wionzcek, Praeger, London, 1966. V. L. Urquidi, *Free Trade and Economic Integration in Latin America*, University of California Press, Berkeley and Los Angeles, 1962. ECLA, *The Latin American Common Market*, UN Sales No. 59.II.G.4, New York, 1959. S. B. Linder, *Trade and Trade Policy for Development*, Praeger Series on International Economics and Development, New York, 1967. C. A. Cooper and B. F. Massell, 'Toward a General Theory of Customs Union for Developing Countries', *Journal of Political Economy*, 73, 461–76, October 1965.

[5] For example, A. Hazlewood, 'The East African Common Market: Importance and Effects', *Bulletin of the Oxford Institute of Economics and Statistics*, February 1966, and 'The Shiftability of Industry and the Measurement of Gains and Losses in the East African Common Market', *Bulletin of the Oxford Institute of Economics and Statistics*, May 1966.

This brings us to the point of stating our own position and foreseeing the course of this paper. It is undoubted that the standard customs union theory is far too narrow for developing countries, but the new customs union theory appropriate to less-developed countries is itself partial and scrappy and needs yet more elements of development theory injected into it. First, one must generalize the idea of customs union from the two or three forms we are used to, i.e. free trade area without deflection rules, free trade area, and customs union —and we must think of a multiplicity of different arrangements involving preferential tariffs either product by product or country by country both within the union and towards outside countries. Next, the evaluation criteria cannot be confined to trade, since the imperfections in these economies are such as to inhibit maximum attainable growth through the unhampered working of national and international markets; we must add in an evaluation on account of industrialization, foreign exchange, savings and other features conducive to development.

The course of our argument can be built on the Cooper and Massell article, but extending this both in analysis and scope. When we have done this, we can look back and we shall find that we are also more broadly based than the Linder approach. We shall see that those writers have gone some way towards escaping from the confines of the old customs union theory, but not far enough.

Cooper and Massell break with what Linder calls the neo-classical customs union theory which views any increase in union national incomes through increased specialization as good, and any impairment of national income through trade diversion as bad. For a less-developed country may value industrialization so much that it is willing to give up a certain amount of achievable national income for this end. That is to say, $1 worth of home-produced industrial output is weighted as more valuable than $1 worth of imports of industrial product, a weighting which market pricing does not reflect. This is especially so for the first few home industrial projects to be established, but a less-developed country may be willing to give up smaller and smaller amounts of national income for further

B

expansions of home industry. These ideas give rise to a supply curve of industrial production as a function of the national income foregone. There is a marginal cost of industrialization in terms of lost income. To the supply analysis is added a demand curve which is supposed to express the central authorities' desire for industrialization. At the margin, the 'excess cost' of the nth industry is equal to the 'excess utility' which is derived from the fact that the nth industry's output is home-produced rather than imported.

It should be noted that the argument is so far developed for one less-developed country only and that it implies a set of differential tariffs applied to the various imports of that country. Thus, in itself, it is unrelated to the idea of customs union at all at present.

But let us continue to develop the argument for this one country and allow ourselves an undue amount of flexibility in setting differential tariff rates (which would be unrealistic if this country had to form agreements with other countries). The main thing is to extend this interesting approach to other elements of development theory.

The first extension is to use the same analysis for the Urquidi–Mikesell–Kitamura–Linder view on foreign exchange saving. Now in this case the losses in possible national income through trade diversion are counter-balanced by import substitution to save foreign exchange. Can this be presented in the same way as the Cooper and Massell industrialization case? Only in principle. We do not need to be confined to industrial production for import substitution, for other types of goods and services may be high yielding in foreign exchange saved. Further, the demand side is more complicated in that different home industries will vary not only in the 'cost' or income foregone, but also in the marginal benefit arising from foreign exchange saved.

Now, similar criticisms could be made of the Cooper–Massell industrialization case. Industrialization is only a cipher for growth-promoting activities through linkages, increase in entrepreneurship, growth of changed attitudes towards effort, etc., and may include a wide variety of activities. But let us integrate the industrialization and foreign exchange cases, since it is true that less-developed countries will in the main wish to substitute imported manufactured goods in order to promote both home industry and foreign exchange saving. But the difficulty we find in applying the demand analysis to the foreign exchange case does produce dissatisfaction with that aspect of the Cooper–Massell industrialization case. For just as each home activity established for foreign exchange saving involves both a differential cost in income foregone and differential benefit in foreign exchange saved, so must each activity established for industrialization carry both a differential cost and differential benefit in growth promoted. In other words, the use of the analysis of Cooper–Massell allows of no differentiation of benefits industry by industry, on the demand side; the differentiation occurs only on the cost side.

Thus instead of ranking home activities by cost as they do, we would rank them by a cost–benefit ratio which will give an entirely different ranking. The replacement of the simple Cooper–Massell supply and demand analysis by the cost–benefit approach has several further advantages. It gets rid of their vague and unmeasurable idea of a central planner's demand curve. For if the cost of the various industries is measurable under the Cooper–Massell approach, so to a certain extent will be the benefits (perhaps more easily in the case of foreign exchange saved). A decision rule as to how much home activity to promote can be turned into a clearer and simpler rule, such as 'protect all home activities where the benefit–cost ratio exceeds 1' instead of trying to operate with a central planner's demand curve. Further, our analysis allows the aggregation of the industrialization and foreign exchange approaches where, following the Cooper–Massell system, different demand curves would have to be applied. Against the cost of establishing any home activity, the benefits of both industrialization and foreign exchange saving must be balanced.

We are now ready to extend the analysis further, still for one country and therefore only as a starting point for the linking of customs union theory and development theory.

For example, just as the total foreign exchange gap of a less-developed country can be reduced differentially by establishing home industries with the greatest foreign exchange savings, so can the savings gap, from which these countries usually suffer, be reduced differentially by the establishment of activities which either use least capital or yield most savings. Concentrating on their production side, this gives a new item, minimizing capital requirements per industry, to be included in the objective func-

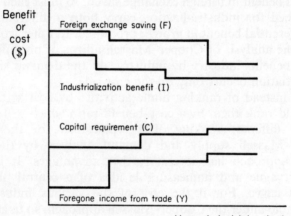

FIG. 1

tion of the cost–benefit appraisal of trade diversion. It is perhaps best entered on the cost side of the account, with the losses from foregone trade.

We arrive at four Cooper and Massell-type 'supply of home activity' curves which appear as in Figure 1. Each curve measures (declining) benefit or (increasing) cost as home industry is developed, sector by sector, in replacement of imported products.

This accounts in a possibly measurable way for the pre-occupation with, and mode of analysis of, less-developed countries, in terms of the savings gap and the foreign exchange gap, and covers the industrialization issue of Cooper and

Massell and the trade side of conventional customs union theory.

It is arguable whether one should go on to include some more elements of development theory. For example, the differential potential for economies of scale in the different home activities above, which has until recently been the only economic argument permitted to less-developed countries to opt out of free

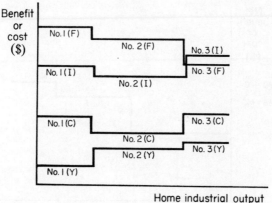

Benefit or cost ($)

Home industrial output

Fig. 2

trade, is not explicitly taken into account: they are all infant industries in the graph and some are going to become sturdier adults than others. Again, the different industries will have different linkage effects through the economy, promoting either 'balanced' or 'unbalanced' growth, according to one's predilections. It is probably better to deal with these real issues in development by examining more closely what is meant by, and what are the supposed benefits of, industrialization, which is at the moment left as a rather diffuse objective.

Returning to Figure 1, it must be carefully noted that home activities on corresponding sections of the supply curves are *different* industries. The industries can be reorganized on a sequential basis, taking one supply curve as a starting point, and a total cost–benefit, or net cost aggregate curve constructed as in Figures 2 and 3.

The cut-off point is then determined by a cost–benefit decision rule rather than by reference to a Cooper–Massell-type demand curve which will be difficult to interpret, and impossible to measure.

The rule allows us to arrive at a differentiated set of tariffs for this single country. In terms of conventional customs

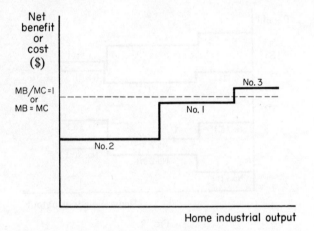

FIG. 3

union theory, we have not touched on trade creation at all yet, but only modified the conventional view that trade diversion is bad by an evaluation procedure which ranks it as desirable or undesirable for a particular less-developed country product by product, and trading country by trading country.

On introducing two countries, and the possibility of forming some kind of customs union or free trade area, the preceding analysis of *trade diversion* is somewhat modified, and we need also to take account of *trade creation*.

Each of the potential union partners has an aggregate supply of industry curve as in Figure 4. It will differ as regards composition of industries, and the length of the 'steps' in the curves will differ, unless we make the Cooper–Massell assumption that the domestic demand is the same for each industrial product in each country. Let us assume this at present.

We now separate out those industries which appear in *both* aggregate supply curves up to the cut-off point. The country with the 'least-cost' production (in terms of the cost–benefit calculus, not conventional cost accounting) now produces for both union partners. This is the analogue of *trade creation*; duplication of production in both countries, where one is 'inferior', is eliminated.

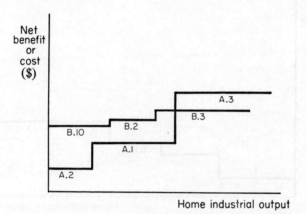

FIG. 4

The tariff required to protect this two-country industry is based on conventional cost (as an excess over the world supply price) in the country in which it has been decided to locate the industry.

Thus, for 'common' industries, country A has industry A2, B has B3. The individual country supply curves are re-formed in Figure 5: and the columnar areas between dotted and full lines are the savings in 'excess cost' of home output, and hence a measure of *trade creation* due to the formation of the customs union. A somewhat different set of tariffs is required in respect of these 'common' industries than in the single-country case: the lowest tariff which would have been required to protect the industry in either A or B is sufficient for the whole union.

The only complication here is that one country may be more 'efficient' (on cost–benefit grounds) in all common industries. Then an arbitrary decision may be needed by the two governments to forego some possible potential joint national income through trade creation for an equitable distribution of industries. The 'loss' of trade creation would be measured by the obliteration of one or more columnar areas.

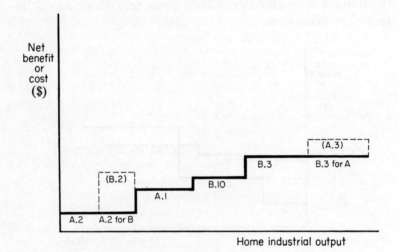

FIG. 5

The other industries in the two separate 'supply' curves, set up by tariffs against the outside world by *diverting trade* (gainful *trade diversion*), remain in the same countries after union. The only difference is that if the countries can both agree to operate the tariff required by one, then each country's industry obtains an expansion of its market. There is potential gain here, but not as yet analysable so long as we continue to assume constant cost industries.

We should look a little more closely at the set of tariffs implied by the union for the various industrial arrangements discussed above.

If we wanted to confine the institutional arrangements to those of a conventional customs union, several problems arise.

Free trade between the partners may raise the problem of an unacceptable share-out of common industries. Then the common external tariff will have to be set at the highest level consistent with protecting the least-acceptable industry in the least 'efficient' country, and may therefore 'protect' undesired (cost exceeds benefit) industries in the partner country.

Thus whilst a conventional customs union does bring gain through both trade creation and trade diversion, it also involves a 'loss' (compared with the optimal situation) on account of negative or injurious *trade creation* (because it may disrupt the desired country distribution rules) and negative *trade diversion* (setting-up of industries behind tariff protection where the costs outweigh the benefits).

As the customs union expands beyond two countries these problems are likely to be exacerbated.

Hence, as opposed to conventional customs union theory, which counts *trade creation* as beneficial and *trade diversion* as harmful, *each* has to be separated into constituent beneficial and harmful parts. A free trade area would still give rise to possibly harmful *trade creation*, but since each country determines its own external tariffs, each could individually cease industrialization when the limit (by its own decision rule) had been reached and not be forced into 'harmful' *trade diversion*. However, if each country sets its own external tariff at the level determined by its own industrialization programme, there will be fewer common industries, and somewhat less scope for *trade creation* than in the customs union case.

The customs union (or free trade area) theory outlined here differs essentially from the conventional theory in that *trade creation* may have beneficial and harmful components to the welfare of the union as a whole, and so may *trade diversion*.

To maximize the beneficial effects requires, in the case of *trade creation*, the establishment of common industries in the 'least-cost' partner (cost as measured in the cost–benefit calculation), but a limit to this policy if one partner is thereby denuded of all industry. The limit is enforced by some kind of protectionism, tariffs or quotas, within the union. Thus the new customs union theory of Linder,[6] which combines free trade within the union of less-developed countries with protection of industries from outside competition, is not quite appropriate. In addition to the possible necessity of some restrictions on internal union trade, the criterion for selection of home industries to be protected has been considerably expanded. Recall that, for Linder, it was based on foreign exchange saving through import substitution.

The expanded criterion is, of course, the criterion for distinguishing beneficial from harmful *trade diversion*. We have built on Cooper and Massell's interesting approach, but integrated and supplemented their industrialization and Linder's foreign exchange benefits of home industrial activity.

What we must now investigate is the possibility of a statistical implementation of this new-style approach to customs union or free trade area theory, corresponding to the empirical side of conventional customs union theory.

[6] S. B. Linder, *Trade and Trade Policy for Development*, Praeger Series on International Economics and Development, New York, 1967.

Chapter 2

QUANTITATIVE ASPECTS OF THE THEORY

Since conventional customs union theory is entirely concentrated on trade, its empirical implementation consists of calculations of the changes in trade consequent upon the rearrangements of tariffs as the customs union or free trade area is formed. We shall review the conventional approach in the empirical analysis as we did in the preceding non-empirical section, but mainly as a basis for suggesting modifications and extensions appropriate to less-developed countries; these extensions on the empirical side should match up as closely as possible to those on the qualitative side.

In the standard empirical approach, three groups of effects on trade from tariff rearrangement are considered.

Direct effects involve trade expansion (contraction) as a tariff cut (increase) reduces (raises) the price of imports relative to home production, and causes a substitution of domestic expenditure away from home production to imports (or vice-versa).

Discriminatory effects of customs union may involve trade expansion between a tariff-cutting group of countries by diverting trade from third countries, against whom tariffs may be increased, to themselves.

Income effects arise from the increase in national incomes due to the increased exports implied by the direct and discriminatory effects.

Generally, the direct effects will be of most significance,

27

discriminatory and income effects being of secondary order of importance.

The measurement of the direct effects, where the price change due to tariff changes is dP/P and imports are originally M_0, is obtained from the import demand curve elasticity.

$$dT = \eta \cdot dP/P \cdot M_0$$
$$= \eta \cdot kt/(1+kt) \cdot M_0$$

where t = the *change* in tariff rate as percentage of original price, and k is the proportion of tariff change passed on to a price change.[1]

Each element in the formula requires some discussion. If we assume 'complete specialization' (no home production), the elasticity estimate will, at one and the same time, cover the *total* domestic demand for the product and be the *import* elasticity of demand for the product.

It can be obtained by regressions of imports and price movements over time for commodity groups or commodities in general. The volume of imports is taken as a function of import prices, P_M, in relation to home prices, P_W. This accounts for the fact that movements in all prices, home and imported, may occur and this would obviously not have a substitution effect on imports.

It may be useful to include the effects on imports of a growth trend in national income, Y, and possibly in foreign exchange reserves, F:

$$Q_M = f(P_M/P_W, Y, F)$$

If quarterly data are available, rather than annual data, a dummy variable to account for the seasonal variation should also be included.

The elasticity estimate thus obtained is a 'consolidated' price elasticity; that is to say, it is unknown whether the factor behind the price change is a tariff change, a tax change, or a change in market conditions. Many writers wish to distinguish such a

[1] $dP/P = (P_t - P_o)/Pt$
$= P_o(1+kt) - P_o/P_o(1+kt)$
$= kt/1+kt.$

price elasticity from a tariff elasticity. A tariff elasticity is expected to be larger than an 'ordinary' price elasticity. The difference is supposed to be due to a 'permanency' effect: importers regard tariff changes as permanent and react by fundamental readjustments, whilst price changes are more likely to be regarded as temporary.[2]

As regards the shifting coefficient, k, in work concerning developed countries either complete shifting has been assumed ($k = 1$) or, in the case of imports from European full-employment economies, one-third of the tariff fall has been absorbed by European exporters facing increasing costs (so that $k = 2/3$ for the price fall in the importing country).[3] Absorption of part of the tariff cut by domestic importers as increased profits (requiring some monopoly power) has been ignored. In conditions of developing countries, with short-run inelasticities of supply on the part of exporting countries, and imperfectly competitive conditions among importers in the importing country, k, may be quite low.

Regarding the relative change in the tariff, it is simple enough to translate the percentage points change in the tariff into appropriate relative terms, t, for use in the formula. But great problems attach to the estimation of tariff level before and after the change. For a group of products, the tariff stated may be an unweighted nominal mean, a weighted nominal mean, or an 'effective' rate of tariff for the group.

Controversy exists as to the relative merits of unweighted and weighted nominal tariffs. In the unweighted case, very high tariffs on minor imports considerably influence the average level of tariffs, which seems unsatisfactory. But then, it is possible that the imports of this commodity *would be* very important were it not for the restrictive effect of the extremely high tariff. Weighted nominal tariffs are complicated by the appropriate weights to use. Usually, the weights are the import values of the commodities, which implies that the average tariff

[2] See D. Dosser, S. S. Han and T. Hitiris, 'Trade Effects of Tax Harmonization: Harmonization of the Value-Added Tax in EEC', *Manchester School*, December 1969.

[3] See B. Balassa and Associates, *Studies in Trade Liberalization*, Johns Hopkins Press, Baltimore, 1967.

included in the calculation in each case is duty proceeds over value of imports as base.

The 'effective' rate of tariff on a product is a fairly new concept.[4] It has been calculated thus. Given a sector of industry producing a given product, essentially one estimates its value-added with the system of tariff protection in existence, compared with the value-added that would exist under free trade. The calculation is implemented by use of input–output tables. The value-added under protection can be simply read off these, since the prices underlying the value of inputs and outputs incorporate tariffs:

$$V'_j = S'_j - \Sigma_i M'_{ij}$$

where V'_j is 'protected' value added for industry j, and S'_j is 'protected' domestic value of output of industry j, and M_{ij} is 'protected' domestic value of inputs purchased by industry j from industry i. The difficulty now occurs in postulating equivalent free trade V_j, S_j and M_j. The simple assumption is made that all tariff changes are reflected entirely in prices, so that:

$$S_j (1 + t_j) = S'_j$$
$$M_{ij} (1 + t) = M'_{ij}$$

V_j, value-added under free trade, is now computed with these *reduced* prices and compared with V'_j. Thus:

the 'effective' rate of tariff $= V'_j - V_j / V_j$.

Of course, the incidence assumption used in what few calculations of 'effective' tariffs have been performed conflicts with any previous assumption that $k \neq 1$.

Let us list the time series required for this exercise of calculating trade effects, which is the conventional empirical counterpart to conventional trade theory. In doing so we shall find that we can utilize the data for partial empirical implementation of the more extended customs union theory for developing coun-

[4] See, e.g. B. Balassa, 'Tariff Protection in Industrial Countries: An Evaluation', *Journal of Political Economy*, 73 (December 1965), and W. M. Corden, 'The Structure of a Tariff System and the Effective Protective Rate', *Journal of Political Economy*, 74 (June 1966).

tries that we have developed earlier, although further statistical work is necessary to complete it.

The elasticity estimates require time series data on import quantities, import values, and import average values, either in the aggregate or by commodities. Price data on home production are required for import prices in relation to home prices, again in aggregate or for the same commodities. If income and foreign exchange reserves are included in the regression, data on these or their proxies are also necessary. These time series will take the form of annual data for ten years or more, or quarterly data for a shorter period, the latter being greatly preferable because of a smaller probability of structural change of the parameters. Many problems may arise, such as the use of fairly unsatisfactory proxies, e.g. production indices for national income and wholesale price indices for retail prices. Also, there may be difficulty in matching up the commodity classification for import quantities and for the price data.

A set of tariff changes for implementation of the basic formula requires information on the pre-union tariff levels and the actual or proposed hypothetical tariff situation after union. A decision has to be made about the use of weighted or unweighted nominal, or effective, rates of tariff. And the commodity classification for tariffs has to be matched up with that used in the import price data.

Finally, the basic pattern of imports is required, and this can be expressed as a matrix of inter- and extra-territorial trade before the formation of the union.

The whole exercise is carried out for a list of products which form the principally traded products for the members of the potential customs union. In the case of a union between developed economies, the work can be done for very broad categories of SITC, i.e. one- or two-digit categories. But when a group of underdeveloped countries is concerned, a listing of the principal imports involves a sundry selection of three digit SITC commodities.

The whole pattern of trade changes, some of which are *trade creation* and some of which are *trade diversion*, can then be ascertained by application of the basic formula to the data mentioned here. Let us assume that we have performed this exercise for a group of less-developed countries, as indeed we have for the selected Caribbean countries studied later in this volume. What we now ask is: what is the statistical programme implied by the proposed 'new-style' customs union theory for developing countries, and to what extent can the conventional statistical exercise be incorporated in and utilized for the new approach.

Let us recall the costs and benefits by which each possible home protected industry is to be evaluated. A possible industry of this type will be one that does not exist at home, but one where the possibility of creation behind a protective wall is feasible (this rules out an imported product dependent on a natural resource which no country in the potential union possesses). For each potential industry there are two costs: (i) national income foregone by protectionism in the Cooper–Massell sense, and (ii) the cost in terms of using up scarce capital resources. There are two benefits: (i) the saving of scarce foreign exchange, and (ii) the development benefits of industrialization.

We should realize that we are dealing with a fundamentally different calculus than conventional national accounting and ordinary cost accounting. Cost consists of a weighted sum of the extra costs involved arising from the relative inefficiency of a sector in the union producing this product *and* the use of scarce home savings which would not otherwise be used for home production. The benefits on account of foreign exchange saving and industrialization are additions to 'welfare' which would not appear in conventional national accounting. For products inside the margin of the cost–benefit decision rule, the weighted sum of the welfare benefits exceeds the weighted sum of the costs; at the margin the two are equal.

For a given potential industry then, the two cost elements can be evaluated in a common unit, namely the local currency. If we keep to the Cooper–Massell assumption for the moment that the import of a product is substituted by an equi-sized home industry, the first cost is given by the size of that import or industry (unit quantity) times the size of tariff needed to protect it (expressed as a percentage of the world supply price) and therefore in money terms. The second element of cost, call on home savings, is determined from information on the fixed and variable capital requirements of the industry in question.

On the benefit side, the saving in foreign exchange is fairly easily handled. As a first approximation, it is the value of imports minus the value of imported inputs required for the new home industry. However, the scarcity of foreign exchange may vary from currency to currency; this can be taken care of by using adjusted exchange rates to convert from the saving in hard or soft currencies into values expressed in the home currency. A measure of the second benefit, stemming from industrialization *per se*, is the most intractable. It may involve employment creation, urbanization, development of linkages in the economy, and external economies. A method would be to use 'direct employment' creation as an indicator of this second benefit, and this is done in Part III.

Now there is a major flaw in the Cooper–Massell approach, really an illegitimate assumption, which greatly affects the evaluation of costs and benefits and must be tackled before any such empirical work takes place. This is the calculation of the prospective size of a home industry which would produce import substitutes. It will be clear that a separate industry (i.e. one which remains particular to a country and does not go into the pool of common industries to be shared out) will not operate on the same scale as the size of imports of that product would indicate, both because of an adverse price effect and an adverse income effect. Common industries would not operate on a scale equivalent to the pre-union imports into the whole union, for the same reasons, although the product of the common industry established in one of the union countries may exceed the pre-union imports of that product into that country. This change in scale from the size of pre-union imports to the extent of post-union home industry will seriously affect the measured costs and benefits of potential import substitution.

The projected size of a home industry producing import substitutes can be roughly determined from the regressions calcula-

C

ted to determine price and income elasticities of demand in the standard empirical work. It is only after this has been done that the development cost–benefit analysis should be applied.

Let us look at separate or non-common industries first and common industries thereafter, from this point of view. The situation for separate industries, continuing to assume constant costs throughout, is represented in Figure 6. Import sector volume for this particular commodity is represented by OQ_1 in

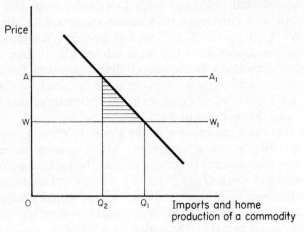

FIG. 6

Figure 6 purchased at the import supply price of WW_1. The supply price of the product in country A is represented by AA_1. Let us assume the tariff has to be set a little above this to preserve the home market for the home industry, and that world exporters will supply none at this price since they can dispose of the product formerly exported to this country at the world supply price to other purchasers.

There is now both a price effect and an income effect against the formerly imported product. Each of these effects can be roughly ascertained from the price demand curve and the income demand curve which are implicit in the demand regressions calculated. The two effects are inter-dependent but let us simplify by considering the price effects first and a subsequent income effect. Because of the less than perfectly inelastic demand curve, the size of home industry will be OQ_2. (Cooper–Massell implicitly assume that the demand is perfectly inelastic.) This involves a national income loss, measured in conventional national accounting, if the demand curve has an elasticity of more than 1 over the relevant range, and a national

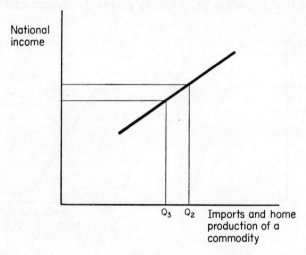

National
income

Q₃   Q₂   Imports and home
production of a
commodity

Fig. 7

income increase if it is less than 1. However, there is always a welfare loss, as measured by the shaded triangle. This follows the usual formula that the welfare loss is the foregone quantity of the product that would be consumed at a non-tariff or 'free-market' price times the size of the tariff divided by two. This is simply the obverse of the standard measure of the welfare gains from trade on the removal of a tariff. It is this welfare loss which can be used as a measure of the real income foregone due to the production of this product inefficiently at home behind tariff walls instead of importing it. And it is this real income loss which should be carried over to the second graph, Figure 7, which will yield a further diminution in the quantity of this product consumed according to the income elasticity of demand for the product in question. Ignoring further repercussions, we can say that the size of the home industry for this product will be approximately OQ_3.

When we turn to common industries the position is more complicated. It can be illustrated by Figures 8 and 9; in the former the price demand curves for countries A and B, in respect of a common product are graphed together and aggre-

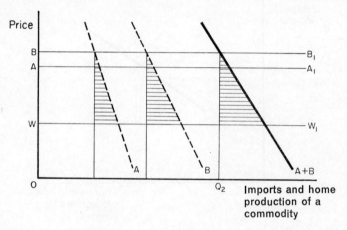

FIG. 8

gated into a union demand curve. It will be seen that one country will eventually produce the required quantity for both partners, OQ_2, before consideration of the income effect, and that this industry will be located in the country which best meets the development cost–benefit criteria. It is most important to emphasize that this may not be the same country which appears to be most efficient on the ground of conventional cost accounting. In Figure 8 the industry has been deliberately located in country B which is somewhat less efficient than A in terms of supply price, considering only conventional cost accounting. The welfare or real income loss is again the shaded area under the $A + B$ curve shared out between the countries A and B according to the shaded areas underneath their curves. (Of course, the real income loss is greater through location in B but it is implicitly assumed that B's lower rating on this is outweighed by other items in the cost–benefit evaluation.) There is a further cutback in the size of the common industry according to this real income loss, and an idea of this can be obtained from the aggregated income demand curve for *A* and *B*, as in Figure 9.

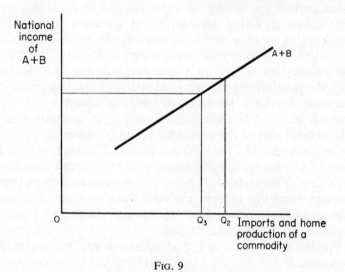

FIG. 9

We can now go on to evaluate the projected separate and common industries, at size OQ_3, for the other items in the development cost–benefit analysis, carrying the real income loss from the abandonment of trade into the total evaluation. It is again best to consider separate and common industries one at a time.

For a separate industry we must now add the further cost item to the real loss above of a worsening of the savings gap in the developing country concerned. The different potential industries will exhibit different capital intensities, both as regards fixed capital involved in setting up industries and variable capital in operating them. Such information might be obtainable from technological data concerning the setting up of similar industries, such as cotton textiles, in other developing countries. Strictly speaking, the capital cost of provision of necessary infrastructure, possibly by public authorities, should be included. It is the social, not private, cost of capital which is relevant.

In the case of a common industry, it is a debatable point as to whether the capital cost should be assigned solely to the union partner possessing the industry. Strictly speaking, we are still assuming factor immobility of customs union theory. Thinking more of a common market, the establishment of a union capital market may make union savings available to any one country for setting up a common industry. But this opens up wider possibilities which would be incorporated in a theory of common markets between developing countries. For the present, let us count the capital cost of a common industry on the debit side of the particular country's account.

On the credit side, the saving of foreign exchange on establishment of a home industry, separate or common, can be measured as: value of imports OQ_1 plus any other reduction in imports through lowering of real national income minus the import content of home production OQ_3, minus the import content of required social overhead capital.

Finally, the benefits of industrialization are the most difficult to measure, but are the chief item in mind when *contra-trade* industrialization measures are undertaken in less-developed countries. It might be more satisfactory to count the three preceding items, foregone national income, use of capital resources, and foreign exchange saving, as short-run and measurable, and 'industrialization' as long-run and diffuse. The trouble with this approach is that the short-run calculus will probably always give a negative answer applying the cost–benefit rule to the setting-up of a home industry (though the weights may prevent this). One solution would be to make the cost-benefit criterion for acceptance of an industry greater than one, which implicitly assigns a *general* benefit arising from the establishment of that industry at home. If this 'excess over unity' rule is made a declining function of the number of home industries, this is equivalent to the Cooper–Massell position (on industrialization alone, of course), but the criticism of giving differential benefits made earlier then applies: it ought to be a function of the particular industry in mind, as well as of the number already established. So whilst recognizing that a general benefit is present, one might attempt to vary this benefit according to the linkages and perhaps skills generated by a new industry—a few discrete variations in the 'excess over unity' rule are permitted.

Thus the *test* for the establishment of a potential industry in the union is as follows:

First question: is it feasible or is it 'specialized' to a country of the outside world due to a unique resource requirement? This will rule out some primary imports, like oil (though the specialist country might be a union partner) and favour secondary processing of primary products, manufacturing, and possible services.

A candidate industry is then evaluated for each union partner according to the anticipated industrialization benefits (I), national income loss (Y), foreign exchange saving (F), and use of capital resources (K). That is, there is a welfare (W) gain or loss from the establishment of the industry, calculated by:

$$\Delta^W = \Delta^I - \Delta^Y + \Delta^F - \Delta^K.$$

If the industry satisfies the criteria, however finally stated for one of the partners, it has the green light; if for more than one, it is 'assigned' to that country with the largest I, but now subject to 'distribution' weights to safeguard against total concentration in one country.

Once weighting is allowed on these grounds, one more complication presents itself. Either for a single country, or for each seen as a union partner, the capital cost and foreign exchange benefit may need to be differentially treated (country by country) according to whether savings or foreign exchange is considered the main brake on development, that is, whether the ex ante 'savings gap' or 'foreign exchange' gap is the dominant gap at the existing stage of development.[5]

[5] See Chenery and Strout, 'Foreign Assistance and Economic Development', *American Economic Review*, September 1966.

Certainly, it would seem that where countries in the union differed in this respect, it should affect the distribution of industries between them according to the 'worst' gap: the dominant gap is given the heaviest weight.

Let us sum up the data requirements and availabilities for the application of this formula in a customs union between developing countries. We should distinguish microeconomic data (at the commodity or industry level) from macroeconomic. 'Standard regressions' mean those made to assess the trade effects of customs union following conventional theory and empirical work for customs unions.

MICROECONOMIC

(i) Size of the home industry given by standard regressions.
(ii) Real national income loss, given by standard regressions.
(iii) Foreign exchange saving: initial value of saving of imports given by data used in standard regressions; import content of the industry and of its social overhead capital would require new data.
(iv) Capital cost, private and social: would require new data.
(v) Tariffs required for protection: from standard regressions.

MACROECONOMIC

(i) Weights to be assigned to national income loss would be given by distribution policy of the union.
(ii) Weights relating to foreign exchange and capital cost could be obtained either from individual development plans or the survey of the development prospects of most less-developed countries continuously under way by UN agencies.

It appears that 'standard regressions' take us a long way in determining the value or otherwise of customs unions between developing countries. The main obstacle would appear to be other micro-data, involving the import and capital content of specific industries; the macro side involving the 'savings versus foreign exchange' gap would not seem so difficult.

In ending our discussion of *customs unions*, we may briefly refer back to our starting point—conventional customs unions and customs union theory.

A major difference in the approach here is the necessity of examining each sector (commodity) in turn. The result may be maintenance of 'free trade' with the outside world for some sectors, free trade with one's union partners for others (common industries). Thus our 'customs union' looks very unlike a conventional one, which prescribes a *carte blanche* rule for free trade within the union and a common external tariff around the union. Nor is it like Linder's version for less-developed countries, which is neo-classical in demanding unrestricted trade within the union, i.e. distribution of industry according to simple comparative advantage.

This brings us to the final and most important difference from the conventional and Linderian approach: the sector-by-sector examination is done by a 'development calculus' which gives an essentially different answer concerning the gains from customs union between developing countries from that which conventional comparative cost would give, or Linder's foreign exchange and Cooper and Massell's industrialization methods would produce.

Trade creation and *trade diversion* are misleading terms in the context of less-developed countries, deriving as these terms do from conventional comparative cost theory. What a customs union of the style outlined here is maximizing is *development creation* not *trade creation*, and minimizing *development diversion* which means *diverting* development potential to an already developed country.

Part II

A CASE STUDY OF CARIBBEAN COUNTRIES

Chapter 3

ECONOMIC CHARACTERISTICS OF
SELECTED CARIBBEAN COUNTRIES

We have chosen five small developing countries of the Caribbean
to study the impact of various integration alternatives within
the frame of reference of the theory developed in Part I. Three
of the five countries are from the British Caribbean: Barbados,
Jamaica, and Trinidad and Tobago; the fourth, Surinam, is a
member of the Tripartite Kingdom of the Netherlands; and
finally the Dominican Republic is a Spanish-speaking independent nation of the region.

Economically, politically, and socially the Caribbean is a
very heterogeneous region. Four different major languages are
spoken in the area and cultural outlook, economic ties, and
consequently the basic economic structures vary according to
the centuries-old past relations with the major European
powers. Within this heterogeneity three criteria have been used
to determine the choice of the five countries: the similarity in
the level of economic development as measured by per capita
output; the freedom in making decisions of possible entry into
various economic groupings, already existing or yet to be
formed; and, perhaps most important of all, the availability
of fairly reliable statistical data in the form required to carry out
with relative accuracy the elasticity and other computations
required for the evaluation of our theory. Thus, readers somewhat familiar with the Caribbean will realize that countries
like Haiti, Puerto Rico, the French West Indies, or the so-called
Little Seven—Associated States with Britain—remain outside
the scope of the analysis by virtue of the criteria. (For instance,
Puerto Rico would qualify with respect to the third criterion,

45

but not with respect to the first two, since it has a comparatively very high per capita income and is not free to make international decisions; Haiti on the other hand would qualify under the second criterion but fail with respect to the first and the third.)

The analysis of the five case studies is rendered somewhat more complex because of their association, or non-association, with major developed economic powers and/or with one another. However, this is all the more interesting with respect to the alternatives possibly open to these countries, since Barbados, Jamaica and Trinidad and Tobago already form part of the Caribbean Free Trade Association (CARIFTA), Surinam is an associate member of the European Economic Community (EEC), and the Dominican Republic, though not a member of any integrated bloc, has a very significant foreign trade with the United States. This last statement applies to the remaining four countries as well, who trade more with the rest of the world than among themselves.

The present chapter is intended to provide the basic economic characteristics of the selected countries. It is neither purely descriptive nor purely analytical, but tries to provide a combination of the two. Unnecessary statistics are avoided and only the essential elements, which are pertinent to later analysis, are pinpointed, namely the existing economic structure, foreign trade relations, and the possible trajectory of the economies.

Although the individual countries show characteristics that are particular to their economies, it can be said generally that, with the exception of the Dominican Republic, they are highly open economies with the ratio of commodity exports and imports to total output exceeding unity. (In the Dominican Republic this ratio is 0·4.) The commodity concentration of exports is very high while imports are very varied. On the other hand both exports and imports are geographically highly concentrated: the few major export products are destined to few major customers and the varied imports are purchased from a few providers, who usually coincide with the customers. All of them have a neglected and underdeveloped agricultural sector which is unable to meet the increasing demand for foodstuffs; and manufacturing, also not generally well-developed, does not go beyond expensive import substitution. With these general remarks we now turn to the individual countries.

I. Barbados (See Tables 3 and 4)

Barbados is the most easterly of the Caribbean islands. Occupied by the British since the early seventeenth century, it was ushered into sovereignty on November 5, 1966.[1] Its geographic area is about 166 square miles. Total population at the end of 1966 was estimated at 250,000, making it the most densely populated country of the region (1,500 individuals per square mile). Income per head is estimated at $400 in 1967.

The most essential economic sector is agriculture. It contributes 25 per cent of the GDP and employs 24 per cent of the labour force. The major crop is sugar; together with its derivatives—molasses and rum—it has been the basis of the Barbadian economy since the seventeenth century. These three products are of paramount importance to the economy in terms of exports. Because sugar cane planting is subject to the vicissitudes of the weather, sugar production is, to a large extent, dependent upon the prevailing climatic conditions and is sometimes very adversely affected. Moreover, by the very nature of cane planting seasonal unemployment is something to be reckoned with. Other agricultural products are milk, livestock, yams, and potatoes, which are wholly consumed on the island. Recently forestry has received some attention.

Manufacturing is insignificant, contributing around 9 per cent of the GDP. It consists mainly of light industries: food and soft drinks, garment, and small metal and wood manufacturing, all of which are import competing and highly labour intensive, which may account for the high share of 14 per cent of the labour force employed in this sector. Of equal importance is the value-added in construction activity—9 per cent—so that manufacturing and construction together contribute 18 per cent of

---

[1] With the breakdown of the West Indian Federation in 1962 Barbados had hoped to stimulate a new federation with itself as head and composed of the Windward and Leeward Islands. The London parley, which was the outcome of this hope, was by and large negative with regard to the realization of the new federation. Barbados became independent.

GDP and employ 26 per cent of the labour force. A paramount rise in construction activity has taken place since 1955, mainly because of the promotion of the tourist industry which has come to be one of the most viable economic sectors of the island. As usual, the economy, with a high degree of openness (exports plus imports/GDP equal 1·06) has a large service sector. Value-added in wholesale and retail trade is 23 per cent of the GDP.

Exports represented 31 per cent and imports 76 per cent of the GDP in 1966. The external trade deficit is not characteristic only of this year but has persisted, rising from BW $23·3 million in 1957 to BW $68·6 million in 1965. Tables 3 and 4 indicate the commodity structure and the geographic direction of trade. Exports consist almost entirely of traditional agricultural products, with sugar and its derivatives constituting 83·4 per cent. The next important item is crustacea—6·8 per cent. Seventy-nine per cent of the sugar is purchased by the United Kingdom at preferential prices determined by the Commonwealth Sugar Agreement. This gives the United Kingdom a prominent role in the geographical direction of exports with a share of more than 55 per cent.

The United States buys only 13 per cent of the exports of Barbados, and this consists of some sugar, molasses and rum, but almost the entire exports of crustacea. Exports to CARIFTA members cannot be considered insignificant with a share of 11 per cent: all exports of lard and margarine and some of rum are directed to them. There is no trade relation with the CACM, and the EEC as a customer practically does not exist.

The import structure is less concentrated both with respect to commodities and geographic direction. In certain items Barbados imports significant amounts from the CARIFTA: all the rice it consumes comes from Guyana, and 25 per cent of petroleum product imports come from Trinidad and Tobago, the remainder almost entirely originating in Venezuela, which gives LAFTA some prominence in imports (10·5 per cent). The United Kingdom and the United States surpass all other geographical areas in providing for the raw material, consumer good, and machinery and equipment needs of Barbados.

II. Jamaica (See Tables 7 and 8)

The island of Jamaica is located in the Caribbean Sea approximately 100 miles south of Cuba and 100 miles west of Haiti. It covers 4,500 square miles of territory. A chain of mountains runs east–west through the central part of the island causing heavy, tropical rainfall in northern regions and drier savannah country in the southern and southwestern plains.

From the middle of the seventeenth century increasing demand from Europe for sugar caused the transformation of Jamaica into a predominantly sugar-producing plantation-type economy and colonial area. In spite of the emancipation of the slaves in 1838, the plantation-based economy was not substantially altered. Although most Negroes moved south from the estates as freemen to farm marginal lands in the mountains and upper valleys, indentured labour was imported from India, adding a new racial strain to the Afro-European population. Later in the nineteenth century sizeable groups of Chinese and Lebanese merchants arrived.

In 1967 the population was 1,893,000 and the population density was 420 persons per square mile. Between 1950 and 1962 approximately 191,000 (net) Jamaicans migrated to foreign countries, in particular to the United Kingdom. This was about 37 per cent of the natural increase in population during the same period, so that migration can be said to have played an important role in relieving population pressure. However, since 1962 the United Kingdom has greatly reduced its quotas for immigrants, and, with prospects dim for other nations to be willing to accept sizeable numbers of immigrants from Jamaica, the population pressures are aggravated.

Since 1950 rapid economic growth has occurred resulting in greatly increased levels of income and output. GDP at factor cost in current prices is presently over $940 million, representing a per capita income of $500. Between 1953 and 1957 the economy expanded rapidly, with GDP rising between 10 and 14 per cent per annum. Since 1957 GDP at constant prices has increased at approximately 4 per cent yearly. The leading sectors of the economy are manufacturing, which contributes roughly

D

15 per cent of gross output, the bauxite–alumina industry which accounts for 10 per cent, and the construction and services— especially tourism—sectors accounting for 25 per cent.

The contribution of the agricultural sector to GDP decreased from 30·8 per cent in 1950 to 11·4 per cent in 1967; yet agriculture is still the activity on which most persons rely for a livelihood. In 1960 approximately 40 per cent of the labour force was employed in that sector, which failed to respond to relatively high demand and prices in export markets during the fifties and early sixties. Furthermore it has not responded to a rising local demand for foodstuffs; thus food prices have risen over 40 per cent since 1955.[2]

The causes of the difficulties encountered in raising productivity in agriculture may be found in the mountainous landscape of the island,[3] the uneconomically small size of the average farm,[4] and the little incentive provided by the system of land tenure for the introduction of improvement by the small farmer. In addition to the existing pattern of landholding, there is further evidence of a relatively poor distribution of income, in spite of high growth rate of the economy.[5]

The manufacturing sector is the largest single contributor to GDP at factor cost among Jamaica's productive sectors. It at present accounts for 15·1 per cent of the total, having increased its relative share from 11·3 per cent in 1950. Since 1950 much diversification has occurred as new manufacturing activities, such as textiles, cement, paints and footwear were begun. The processing of local agricultural products, including rum, sugar, and tobacco has also increased, but at a slower pace than other manufacturing efforts.

[2] The general price level rose by approximately the same amount, with housing costs rising the most—67 per cent—clothing costs the least—18 per cent.

[3] This means that only one-third of its total area, or 1·7 million acres is suited to continuous cultivation.

[4] The 1961/62 agricultural census showed that 71 per cent of the farms were smaller than 5 acres each and constituted only 12 per cent of total farm acreage while 0·2 per cent of the farms were over 500 acres and constituted 45 per cent of total farm acreage. The historical pattern of land distribution has left a few farms with much fertile land and many small farms with marginal land.

[5] See A. Ahiram, 'Income Distribution in Jamaica, 1958', *Social and Economic Studies*, 13:3 (1964), 333–69.

The discovery of bauxite induced a rapid expansion of the mining sector, and its contribution to GDP increased from virtually nothing in 1950 to about 10 per cent in 1967. Nevertheless, due to its primarily foreign ownership and capital-intensive nature, only 50 per cent of the value of output goes to Jamaican residents, and mining employs less than 1 per cent of the labour force.

The principal exports of Jamaica are bauxite, alumina, and sugar, the first two accounting for one-half of the value of domestic exports and sugar accounting for about one-fifth. Other major export commodities are banana, fruit and fruit juices, coffee, pimento, and rum. The United States receives 38 per cent of total exports and buys all the shipments of bauxite, and about one-half of rum. The United Kingdom receives 27·5 per cent, buying the largest share of almost all agricultural exports. Exports to the EEC, consisting primarily of agricultural commodities, are less than 2 per cent of total exports, and both the CACM and LAFTA receive less than 1 per cent of exports. Fruit and fruit juices and coffee are the main exports to CARIFTA which gets 1·3 per cent of Jamaica's total exports.

The most important imported commodities are petroleum and petroleum products, motor vehicles, mining and construction equipment, and iron and steel products. Imports of food products account for about 20 per cent of all imports, with flour and rice being the two most important items. As is expected, a wide variety of manufactured products is imported, the principal ones being chemical materials, paper and paperboard, textiles, and electric machinery. The United States supplies over 30 per cent of Jamaica's imports and the United Kingdom about 25 per cent. The EEC and LAFTA supply 8·3 per cent and 7·9 per cent of total imports. Once again, the high relative share of LAFTA is accounted for by petroleum product imports from Venezuela. The CACM and CARIFTA each supply less than 2 per cent. Unlike the case of other countries, Trinidad and Tobago does not ship petroleum products to Jamaica. CARIFTA's most important single trading partner is Guyana which supplies one-third of Jamaica's rice imports.

Principally due to bauxite and alumina production, there has been a shift in the direction of trade since the fifties. Imports and exports to the dollar area have increased substantially, and the United States and Canada have replaced the United Kingdom as Jamaica's main trading partners, although special marketing arrangements for banana, citrus, and sugar are still maintained with the United Kingdom, which account for the large shipments of these products to this country.

Jamaica's future development will depend greatly on the degree to which exports can be increased. In the past there has been much dependence on special marketing arrangements and little effort at developing new markets for traditional exports. The output of bauxite and alumina is relatively easy to increase, but demand conditions in export markets limit the quantities that can be sold. On the other hand, where export demand is high and relatively elastic, as was the case, for example, for coffee and cocoa during most of the fifties, output has not responded with the result that the value of domestic exports of citrus, coffee, cocoa, pimento, ginger and their products declined from £4·4 million in 1958 to £4·2 million in 1962 and amounted to only £4·5 million in 1967.

III. Trinidad and Tobago (See Tables 1 and 2)

Trinidad and Tobago are the most southerly of the Caribbean islands. Trinidad is about 10 miles from the South American continent and Tobago is approximately 18 miles to the northeast of Trinidad. Trinidad became the property of the British Crown by the Treaty of Amiens in 1802. Tobago was ceded to Britain in 1814, and the administrative centre of the island was transferred to Trinidad around 1888. The islands became independent in 1962 with the breakdown of the West Indian Federation.

The geographical area is 1,980 square miles, of which Trinidad has 1,864 square miles. The total population is slightly over one million and is growing at an annual rate of 3 per cent. Income per head in 1966 was $730, the highest of the five countries.

The country is endowed with some natural resources. There is natural asphalt and petroleum which was first exploited in

1909. It is the single most important activity of the economy, contributing 27·8 per cent of the GDP in 1966. Its relative share in output has been continuously declining since 1957 when it had reached 36·5 per cent; and it only employs 5 per cent of the labour force. Petroleum and petroleum products are also the single most important export item (80 per cent of domestic exports in 1966); however, Trinidad and Tobago does not rely solely on its own resources but imports large quantities of crude and partly refined oil from Venezuela, Colombia, and the Netherlands Antilles, which it then refines and re-exports.

Agriculture is the most important employer—20 per cent of the labour force in 1960—but it contributed in 1966 only 10 per cent of the gross value-added. Until 1931 cocoa was the main crop; it has since then been replaced by sugar. Other agricultural crops are citrus and banana. The relative share of agriculture in GDP has been falling since 1950 and the value-added in this sector—in constant prices—has been stagnant since the middle of the fifties. As a result, foodstuffs are imported in large quantities. One of the gravest problems hindering increases in agricultural output is the dualistic structure of the sector divided into plantation and peasant economies. The latter is characterized by the use of traditional methods of farming with low yields per acre; in the former productivity is higher and its output is oriented towards exports to the United Kingdom.

Despite the promotional activities and the establishment of an industrial development corporation in 1957 to provide the ways and means for the diversification of the economy with emphasis on industry, manufacturing activity has not expanded sizeably in the past decade; it contributes about 14 per cent of the GDP and employs 15 per cent of the labour force. It consists mainly of small enterprises which aim at import substitution and is relatively labour intensive. A few large-scale enterprises are being established and these are mostly capital intensive end-geared towards export markets.

Wholesale and retail trade are just as important as manufacturing in creating income and output, and also employ a significant portion of the labour force—12 per cent. While tourism cannot be said to be a major economic sector, it employs a not insignificant amount of workers and its foreign exchange earnings cannot be ignored. In 1962, the national income content of tourism was estimated to be approximately one-half of the aggregate earnings of this sector.

The principal exports of Trinidad and Tobago are petroleum and petroleum products; as mentioned previously they provide four-fifths of the foreign exchange earned by domestic exports. The remainder consist of traditional agricultural products. One-third of the petroleum products are shipped to the United States, one-tenth to the United Kingdom and another one-tenth to the EEC. Trinidad and Tobago is the major oil supplier to the Caribbean in general and to the CARIFTA in particular. In the latter bloc its largest customer is Guyana, but all members purchase this commodity from Trinidad and Tobago. Among the remaining countries of the Caribbean, the Netherlands Antilles and Puerto Rico are the major customers of this product. It should be added that Canada also buys about 5 per cent and EFTA countries, excluding the United Kingdom, purchase also about one-tenth of the exports of oil. The second major item of export is sugar, practically three-fourths of which is purchased by the United Kingdom under special marketing arrangements. Because of the preponderance of oil products in the export structure and the relatively high share purchased by the United States, almost one-third of the total shipments are directed to this country. Including Canada, dollar area exports represent almost two-fifths of total exports. Exports to CARIFTA are 6 per cent, which is one-fifth of total exports to the Caribbean area in general. Exports to LAFTA and CACM are negligible.

Because of the special position of oil in Trinidad's economy the commodity structure of imports is highly concentrated as well, with crude and partly refined petroleum constituting one-half of total imports. The major source of this raw material is LAFTA, i.e. Venezuela, with a very much smaller amount purchased from Colombia. Excluding oil, the commodity concentration of imports does not differ from that of the other four countries, with motor vehicles, industrial and electrical machinery, iron and steel products having relatively significant shares. Again among the foodstuffs milk, flour, and rice are the most important imported items.

Due to the preponderance of oil refining the geographic concentration is also high, the prominent role played by the United States in the Caribbean in general now giving way to LAFTA. This regional block provides 36 per cent of total imports, the United States and the United Kingdom having similar relative shares (14 and 16 per cent respectively). CARIFTA provides more than nine-tenths of the imported rice, which is the major commodity exported by this integrated bloc to Trinidad and Tobago. Because of special agreements the great bulk of flour comes from Canada. Again imports from the CACM are negligible.

IV. The Dominican Republic (See Tables 5 and 6)

The Dominican Republic embraces the eastern portion of the island of Hispaniola, one of the Greater Antilles located between Cuba and Puerto Rico. The western section of the island is the French-speaking Republic of Haiti. Between 1930 and 1961 the Dominican Republic was dominated politically by the military dictatorship of Rafael Trujillo. The assassination of Trujillo in 1961 ushered in a period of extreme political instability, culminating in a civil war between rival military factions in 1965. Free elections were held in 1966, and since that time the country has slowly been recovering from the economic and political crises of the previous years.

The geographical area is approximately 19,000 square miles. The population in 1966 was 3,750,000, of which over 500,000 is located in the national district surrounding the capital, Santo Domingo. In 1964 approximately 64 per cent of the population was situated in rural areas; yet it is estimated that the urban–rural proportion will change to 50–50 by 1980. The annual rate of growth of the population is 3·6 per cent, and the relative importance of young age groups is indicated by the fact that in 1960 over 50 per cent of the population was less than 20 years old. Per capita income is estimated at $280.

The economy has historically been agriculture-based and remains so to the present, although strenuous efforts are being made to establish industries, principally through import substitution. Agriculture, excluding sugar, accounts for just over 17 per cent of gross domestic product but employs (including fishing) some 55 per cent of the labour force. The most important crop is sugar, virtually all of which is exported to the United States. Other principal agricultural crops are cocoa, tobacco, banana, and coffee. Exports of these five commodities comprise 85 per cent of total exports, and due to their widely fluctuating world market prices cause similar fluctuations in export receipts.

The manufacturing sector, including the sugar industry, accounts for 16·5 per cent of gross domestic product and employs about 12 per cent of the labour force. The sugar industry alone employs 9·2 per cent of the labour force. Excluding the sugar industry, manufacturing accounted for approximately 11 per cent of the GDP in 1966. This indicates the heavy dependence of the country on a single agricultural product as well as pointing up the significance of sugar production and processing as the backbone of the industrial sector. Commerce and government are the other two most important sectors, contributing 18 and 14 per cent of GDP respectively.

GDP at constant market prices rose 29 per cent between 1950 and 1964 and fell slightly between 1964 and 1966 due to the paralysation of economic activity during the civil strife. The decade of the fifties showed an increase in the concentration of income in both industry and agriculture. For example, a doubling of the number small farms of (less than 5 acres) occurred at the expense of the division of small and mechanized farms, while the number of large estates (over 140 acres) increased slightly. The concentration of income in industry has occurred through the growth of businesses in the hands of a limited number of persons. This situation has not been basically altered in the present decade.

Exports consist primarily of traditional tropical agricultural products and bauxite. Sugar, cocoa, tobacco, banana, coffee, and bauxite account for 92 per cent of total exports, with sugar exports alone representing 56 per cent, and coffee 15 per cent. The highly concentrated structure of the geographical direction of exports is revealed in Table 6. The United States purchases 87 per cent: almost the entire exports of bauxite, sugar and its derivatives, and cocoa and its derivatives, and 76 per cent of coffee are shipped to the States, followed by the EEC which takes 6 per cent (tobacco, banana, and coffee). Other economic blocs in the neighbourhood—LAFTA, CARIFTA, and CACM—receive negligible amounts.

Imports, on the other hand, are more varied in both geographical origin and commodities. A wide range of food, manufactured goods, and capital equipment is imported. Chemical and pharmaceutical products, motor vehicles, iron and steel manufactures and construction materials, electrical equipment, petroleum products, cereal grains and dairy products are among the most important imported products. The United States supplies 46 per cent of total imports and the entire supply of wheat and wheat flour. In other imports its share varies between 30 and 40 per cent. The EEC supplies 16 per cent of total imports. Trade with the CACM is inconsequential. CARIFTA and LAFTA supply 2·4 and 2·1 per cent respectively. The major item of import from these blocs is gasoline from Trinidad and Tobago and crude oil from Venezuela.

A surplus in the balance of payments was regularly maintained until 1961. The termination of the Trujillo dictatorship led to greatly increased imports of consumer goods as well as expenditures on travel abroad, both of which were strictly curtailed until that time. As such, the current account has been in deficit since 1962 and is the principal contributor to an overall unfavourable trend in the payments balance during the past few years. An exception occurred in 1965 when large imports to the capital account from abroad caused an overall payments surplus. In general imports are increasing at a greater rate than exports, and the balance of payments deficit is met out of public and private capital imports from abroad. No short-term improvement in the trade balance is foreseen, resulting in a major emphasis on policies regarding the external sector as found in the current development plan (1968–85), so that balance of payments constraints will not impede future economic growth.

V. Surinam (See Tables 9 and 10)

Surinam, formerly Dutch Guiana, is the middle of the three Guianas situated on the northeast coast of South America. Politically it has enjoyed virtual autonomy in home affairs since the early fifties. As of December 29, 1954, it forms part of the Tripartite Kingdom of the Netherlands[6] and as of September 1, 1962, it is an associate member of the EEC. Its ties with the EEC, however, go further than a mere associate membership, since being part of the Kingdom of the Netherlands it receives substantial financial assistance from Holland, who on the whole provides two-thirds of the resources to implement the development plans, partly as loan and partly as grant.

The geographical area is more than 55,100 square miles; but, 80 per cent of this large territory being covered by almost impenetrable jungle, the majority of its population of 335,000 is concentrated in the coastal zone, in and around Paramaribo, the capital. Income per head is estimated at $430 in 1965.

The most important industrial sector is mining. Surinam produces one-seventh of the world output of bauxite. This economic activity contributed nearly 30 per cent of the gross output of the country, but employs only 5 per cent of the labour force. Surinam lays great stress on the exploitation of this mineral of which it has an abundance and in good quality. An alumina beneficiation plant and an aluminium smelter have been in operation since late 1965, and the exports of the processed mineral have been rising at fantastic rates.[7]

Agriculture, which used to be the single most important sector up to well into the period of World War II, today only accounts for 12 per cent of the entire output, but engages one-half of the labour force. The most important crop is rice, which

[6] Formed of Holland, the Netherlands Antilles, and Surinam.

[7] Alumina exports rose from 59,000 metric tons in 1965 to 345,000 metric tons in 1966. Similarly aluminium exports increased from 1,254 to 25,503 metric tons respectively. See Suriname, Ministerie van Financien, *Financiële nota behörende bij de ontwerpbegroting voor het dienstjaar 1968*, Table 21.

is also the major agricultural export commodity (more than one-half of total agricultural exports). It is extremely sensitive to weather changes and its price fluctuates widely in the world market. Hence severe fluctuations in receipts from its exports. Other agricultural crops are banana, cocoa, coffee, sugar, orange, grapefruit, and maize. Forestry, though potentially important, is at present unable to meet even the domestic demand for timber, because of the present state of forests which raises production costs.

Manufacturing, including construction and utilities, employs 14 per cent of the labour force and contributes 18 per cent of the aggregate output. Because of the small size of the domestic market it is confined to either small-scale import substituting consumer goods, or, wherever possible, primarily geared to export. Until recently this meant processing of forestry and agricultural products; since 1966 alumina and aluminium have joined the ranks.

Like all the other countries who provide the case studies of this book, Surinam is an extremely open economy. In 1965 exports of merchandise constituted 40 per cent of the GDP at market prices while imports of commodities were 66 per cent of the aggregate output.[8] Imports have expanded faster than exports and the deficit in the balance of trade has risen from Sf 1·7 million in 1954 to Sf 60·9 million in 1965. Bauxite is the major foreign exchange earner (79·7 per cent of total exports), This is followed by timber (15·4 per cent), fish and fish preparations (2·2 per cent), and paper products (1·7 per cent); the remaining 6·5 per cent consists of agricultural products other than rice.

The geographical direction of exports reveals its highly concentrated structure: 73 per cent are shipped to the United States and 10·3 per cent to the EEC (around three-fourths of this latter share are exports to Holland). LAFTA, in which Surinam could be potentially interested as a member (for which she will meet with no resistance either from Holland or the EEC), is a very insignificant trading partner. The United States buys largely bauxite

---

[8] Although more recent external trade statistics are available, data on aggregate output has not been published after 1965; hence it is impossible to give more recent degrees of openness.

(88 per cent of total shipments), timber (9·1 per cent) and shrimp (54·6 per cent). The EEC buys the greatest share of all the other major export commodities with the exception of timber, fish, and textiles. Surinam does not sell any merchandise to the CACM and exports only insignificant quantities to the CARIFTA.

The commodity structure of imports is very much less concentrated. Although an economic classification is not directly discernible from Table 9 various types of raw materials and investment equipment account for more than two-thirds of total imports. Again the United States is the major provider followed by the EEC, i.e. Holland. CARIFTA members export more to Surinam than they import from her. Among them Trinidad and Tobago is the most significant, providing 90 per cent of Surinam's needs for petroleum products. In fact Trinidad and Tobago provide for 85 per cent of Surinam's aggregate exports from the CARIFTA. LAFTA is an insignificant trading bloc. Once again there are no shipments of merchandise from the CACM to Surinam.

VI. Future policies

Structurally similar, the five countries discussed above also show considerable resemblance in their aspiration towards future economic development.

The Jamaican *Five Year Independence Plan 1963–68*, the first phase of a long-term development programme, takes note of the lack of public services and infrastructure and emphasizes the need for these basic components of industrial development. The sectors whose contribution to gross output is expected to grow fastest are public utilities, transport and distribution, and manufacturing. Within the latter group, the areas of building materials and wood and metal products are expected to expand rapidly.

The strategy of Jamaica's proposed development is one of orientation towards export markets. Foreign manufacturing industries are offered liberal investment incentives and local agricultural production for export is expected to assume an increasingly important role. This strategy is consistent with the fact that Jamaica alone comprises a small market with relatively low effective demand.

Increased imports of both consumption and investment goods, as well as a continual deterioration in the terms of trade, have caused a substantial annual deficit in the current account during the past decade. In 1967 the deficit was £27·6 million. Over the range of the *Plan* period approximately 25 per cent of gross domestic capital formation is financed through capital inflows from abroad, and 60 per cent of government capital formation is financed externally.

Another area of principal concern is the reduction of unemployment, to which government projects are specifically oriented; yet certain structural factors such as a large number of underemployed people and significant internal migrations to urban areas, have impeded the use of specific targets for reductions of unemployment.

Industrialization in Jamaica has been characterized by the development of capital intensive industries (i.e. bauxite) financed principally from abroad, and more recently by efforts to diversify manufacturing output for import substitution. Efforts to distribute new industries outside the urban areas have only just begun, and the continuing dilemma of annual balance of payments deficits remains the overriding consideration in planning.

The present development plan of the Dominican Republic (1968–85), in recognition of the severe balance of payments crisis, emphasizes the promotion and execution of projects having immediate effects on import substitution and foreign exchange receipts. Government expenditures aim to promote exports of traditional agricultural products and self-sufficiency in many agricultural commodities now imported. There is also substantial interest in building a petroleum refinery, again with a view to saving foreign exchange.

Manufacturing industries are foreseen as extensions of a broad agricultural base as, for example, development of a textile industry from raw cotton production, and fruit processing and canning from fruit growing. Although the growth of widely diverse manufacturing industries is not anticipated, the further exploitation of existing natural resources (limestone, bauxite, gypsum, nickel) is deemed appropriate.

The assumed advantages, in terms of growth of income and employment, of heavy investments in manufacturing are foregone in order to induce more efficient and diverse agricultural activities. This is understandable when one considers that the existing strengths of the economy rest in the agricultural sector, primarily in sugar production, in spite of large volumes of food imports and fluctuations in world commodity prices; and that the balance of payments deficit will continue to have a serious restricting effect, both in terms of meeting foreign obligations and impeding investment.

Additional objectives include the elimination of urban–rural income discrepancies and lowering the amount of unemployment. Employment creation is pursued through agricultural reforms in rural areas and public sector investments in infrastructure, housing, and services. Although private foreign investment will clearly play a role in the industrialization scheme, no promotion programmes, such as tax or other incentives, have been utilized beyond the potential tariff protection of new industries until the industrial incentive law of 1968 which concedes to new establishments exemption from taxes on income and from duties on imported raw materials.

The Dominican Republic is the only one of the five Caribbean countries to foresee in its plan future participation in a common market or free trade area in Latin America. This appears to be an implicit rejection of the importance of foregone income due to trade diversion, at least in the longer view; but for the present period these considerations are subordinated to the task of wholesale economic recuperation and rejuvenation through balance of payments reforms and measures to promote productivity and efficiency.

The problems confronting planners in Barbados and Trinidad and Tobago are not markedly different from those in Jamaica or the Dominican Republic. Each country has an annual trade deficit, severe unemployment, and an economy heavily dependent on a few major exports: sugar and tourism in Barbados; oil and oil products in Trinidad and Tobago.

The development plans for each country require foreign financing to the extent of at least 50 per cent. Import substitution and export expansion are important objectives. Barbados stresses substitution in light industries such as food and soft drinks, garments, and small wood manufactures, while at the same time placing emphasis on the development of agriculture as shown by a higher allotment in the plan to agriculture than to industry. Barbados is in this sense similar to the Dominican Republic.

Trinidad and Tobago's historical dependence on oil has lately become a source of concern due to a slowdown in the growth of the industry. Export expansion in manufacturing is undertaken with special emphasis on capital intensive industries in order to counter the potential effects of slower growth in oil. Nevertheless such expansion requires high initial outlays of capital with corresponding effects on the balance of payments. Also, with less emphasis on job creation and more on output and growth, employment is likely to suffer.

The economic structure of Surinam is determined principally by the mining sector, i.e. the production of bauxite and the associated aluminium industry. As in Trinidad and Tobago, this one-industry dependence has led to a desire for diversification of output. Development planning in Surinam, as outlined in the *Ten Year Plan 1966–75*, strives for other familiar objectives including reduction in unemployment and the inequalities in income distribution, equilibrium in the balance of payments, and increases in real income.

Leading sectors in addition to mining are hydro-electric energy, agriculture, forestry, and industry. Since the structure of the economy does not allow for considerable expansion in the domestic market, production of the leading sectors is oriented towards world markets with the aim of raising exports substantially, so that the deficit in the balance of trade can be reduced. Yet the export-oriented industries are highly capital intensive and this technique of production conflicts with the objective of reducing employment. This is an aspect of the plan that the government may be willing to forego for the sake of achieving the desired expansion in output and exports.

For the purpose of reducing income disparities among regions, productive activities in regions outside the capital city are initiated and encouraged; but this objective is in conflict with other objectives, e.g. the rapid expansion of production of goods and services. Because there is at the same time much concern over productivity increases in the *Plan*, it appears unlikely that any effective distribution of industries will occur.

In summary, the industrialization policies of the Caribbean countries under discussion are remarkably similar, springing from related objectives and reflecting common problems. Chronic balance of payment deficits lead to orientation towards external markets and import substitution in an attempt to control receipts and payments, finance investment, promote employment, etc. Government investments are concentrated in those sectors which lead to fastest growth. This varies from the agriculture based philosophy of the Dominican Republic and, to a lesser extent, Barbados, to reliance on capital intensive industrial sectors in Trinidad and Tobago and Surinam. In Trinidad and Tobago the problem is to compensate for the declining oil industry, while in Surinam it is the promotion of the aluminium industry.

The plans of each country invariably include a large reliance on foreign capital to finance development. Further, each country is confronted with the need to create employment, an objective which must be balanced against the need for capital-intensive export-oriented industries, the latter providing both foreign exchange receipts and stimulation for growth. Thus the efforts made at industrial expansion are directed towards the more immediate problem of foreign exchange earning and saving and for the sake of employment promotion rather than being concerned with the idea of foregoing income by producing locally within tariff walls at higher cost. To some extent the benefits of either approach overlap and the distinction as to why one or the other is followed is superfluous; nevertheless prominence is given the overriding need to become less dependent on imports and less distracted by large payments deficits. Yet there is a need for a delicate balance in costs, since high-cost import substitution can be detrimental to potential export oriented industries as well as not redress the balance of payments problem.

The question to be asked at this stage is: to fulfil at least part of their economic aspirations should these five countries join integrated economic blocs so that they may benefit from the advantageous dynamic effects of large-size markets, economies of scale, industrialization etc. ? If so, which should be the block of their choice? The answer to the first question depends on the evaluative procedure outlined in Part I. But we also need to know just what integration schemes are available to them. These are taken up in the next Chapter.

E

Table 1 Trinidad and Tobago. Geographical origin of major import commodity groups, 1966
(US $000)

	USA	UK	EEC	EFTA	CACM	LAFTA	CARIFTA	Other	Total Imports	% Distribution by commodity
Milk and cream	44·4 (0·7)	746·4 (12·5)	1,638·0 (27·4)	364·2 (6·1)	—	7·8 (0·1)	—	3,169·2 (53·2)	5,970·0 (100·0)	(1·3)
Rice	0·6 (—)	—	—	—	—	—	5,187·0 (93·0)	387·6 (7·0)	5,575·2 (100·0)	(1·2)
Flour	812·4 (15·1)	76·8 (1·4)	328·8 (6·1)	—	—	—	—	4,169·4 (77·4)	5,387·4 (100·0)	(1·2)
Petroleum						162,304·2 (70·2)		68,779·8 (29·8)	231,084·0 (100·0)	(49·5)
Petroleum products	375·6 (10·5)	1,692·6 (47·3)	40·2 (1·1)	—	—	978·6 (27·0)	82·8 (2·3)	408·6 (11·8)	3,578·4 (100·0)	(0·8)
Textile fabrics	2,032·2 (30·9)	1,486·8 (22·6)	411·0 (6·2)	22·8 (0·3)	—	3·0 (—)	1·8 (—)	2,627·4 (40·0)	6,585·0 (100·0)	(1·4)
Iron and steel	2,346·0 (15·3)	9,669·6 (63·0)	1,525·8 (8·6)	67·8 (0·4)	—	268·8 (1·8)	1·8 (—)	1,457·4 (9·6)	15,337·2 (100·0)	(3·3)
Manufacturers of metal	2,322·0 (22·3)	4,543·2 (43·6)	1,285·2 (12·3)	227·4 (2·2)	—	34·2 (0·3)	10·2 (0·8)	2,008·2 (19·2)	10,430·4 (100·0)	(2·2)
Industrial machinery	13,795·2 (59·4)	7,299·6 (31·4)	1,268·4 (5·5)	217·8 (0·9)	—	239·4 (1·0)	14·4 (0·1)	408·6 (1·7)	23,243·4 (100·0)	(5·0)
Electrical machinery	5,596·2 (41·6)	4,516·8 (33·6)	1,222·8 (9·1)	147·6 (1·1)	—	55·8 (0·4)	0·6 (—)	1,918·8 (14·2)	13,458·6 (100·0)	(2·9)
Road motor vehicles	528·6 (3·1)	12,483·6 (74·0)	1,447·8 (8·6)	34·8 (0·2)	—	3·0 (—)	1·2 (—)	2,381·4 (14·1)	16,880·4 (100·0)	(3·6)
Manufactured articles	1,497·6 (28·0)	1,442·4 (27·0)	578·4 (10·8)	37·2 (0·7)	—	8·4 (0·2)	44·4 (0·8)	1,737·6 (32·5)	5,346·0 (100·0)	(1·1)
Paper and paper products	1,755·0 (24·8)	2,103·0 (29·7)	356·4 (5·0)	628·8 (8·9)	—	6·6 (0·1)	3·0 (—)	2,233·8 (31·5)	7,086·6 (100·0)	(1·5)
Other	34,988·4 (29·6)	30,002·4 (25·8)	6,917·2 (6·1)	4,505·4 (3·8)	833·4 (0·7)	2,384·0 (1·9)	3,948·6 (3·2)	33,625·2 (28·9)	117,204·6 (100·0)	(25·0)
TOTAL IMPORTS	66,094·2 (14·2)	76,063·2 (16·3)	17,019·6 (3·7)	6,253·8 (1·4)	833·4 (0·2)	166,293·0 (35·9)	9,295·8 (2·0)	125,314·2 (26·5)	467,167·2 (100·0)	(100·0)

Source: Worksheets of a study prepared by F. Andic and S. Andic for the Caribbean Development Project of the Twentieth Century Fund.

Notes
1. BW $1.00 = US $0.60
2. Bracketed figures indicate percentages of total imports.
3. EFTA excludes UK, shown separately.

Table 2 Trinidad and Tobago. Geographical direction of major export commodities, 1966
(US $000)

	USA	UK	EEC	EFTA	CACM	LAFTA	CARIFTA	Other	Total Exports	% Distribution by commodity
Crude petroleum and products	123,663·6 (35·3)	33,539·4 (9·6)	34,232·4 (9·8)	29,799·6 (8·5)	707·4 (0·2)	—	11,698·2 (3·4)	114,927·6 (33·0)	348,568·2 (100·0)	(80·1)
Refined and unrefined sugar	1,390·8 (5·9)	17,308·2 (73·1)	—	—	—	—	784·8 (3·3)	4,200·6 (17·7)	23,684·4 (100·0)	(5·4)
Cocoa beans	1,037·4 (40·5)	761·4 (29·8)	676·2 (26·4)	35·4 (1·4)	—	—	—	48·0 (1·9)	2,558·4 (100·0)	(0·6)
Natural asphalt (dried)	73·8 (3·4)	1,602·0 (74·8)	378·0 (17·6)	12·0 (0·6)	—	—	7·2 (0·3)	69·0 (3·3)	2,142·0 (100·0)	(0·5)
Other	19,868·4 (34·1)	6,604·2 (11·3)	5,713·2 (9·8)	1,393·8 (9·8)	1,703·4 (2·9)	6,012·0 (10·3)	12,112·8 (20·8)	4,813·2 (1·8)	58,221·0 (100·0)	(13·4)
TOTAL EXPORT	146,034·0 (34·2)	59,815·2 (14·0)	40,999·8 (9·6)	31,240·8 (7·2)	2,410·8 (0·6)	6,012·0 (1·4)	24,603·0 (5·8)	124,058·4 (27·5)	435,174·0 (100·0)	(100·0)

Source: Worksheet of a study prepared by F. Andic and S. Andic for the Caribbean Development Project of the Twentieth Century Fund.
Notes
1. BW $1.00 = US $0.60
2. Bracketed figures indicate percentages of total exports.
3. EFTA excludes UK, shown separately

Table 3   Barbados. Geographical origin of major import commodities, 1965
(US $000)

	USA	UK	EEC	EFTA	CACM	LAFTA	CARIFTA	other	Total xs	% Distribution by commodity
Flour	176·5 (13·7)	0·2 (—)	372·3 (28·9)	—	—	1,214·1 (22·7)	—	737·7 (57·3)	1,286·7 (100·0)	1·8
Meat	994·5 (18·6)	124·1 (2·3)	153·7 (2·9)	274·1 (5·1)	—	—	—	2,586·4 (48·4)	5,346·9 (100·0)	7·7
Rice	18·6 (1·4)	—	—	—	—	—	1,351·2 (98·6)	—	1,369·8 (100·0)	2·0
Milk and cream	30·0 (1·5)	314·4 (15·9)	1,026·0 (51·8)	147·1 (7·4)	—	—	—	464·9 (23·4)	1,982·4 (100·0)	2·8
Petroleum Products	169·2 (2·7)	76·8 (1·2)	9·6 (0·2)	—	—	4,435·2 (70·0)	1,584·6 (25·0)	59·4 (0·9)	6,334·8 (100·0)	9·1
Feeding stuff for animals	583·8 (33·8)	34·8 (2·0)	—	13·7 (0·8)	—	522·0 (30·3)	53·4 (3·1)	517·3 (30·0)	1,725·0 (100·0)	2·5
Textile fabrics	504·6 (32·7)	313·2 (20·3)	45·0 (2·8)	15·4 (1·0)	—	—	1·8 (0·1)	660·8 (43·0)	1,540·8 (100·0)	2·2
Iron and steel	90·6 (5·9)	943·8 (61·5)	82·8 (5·4)	9·7 (0·6)	—	—	6·0 (0·4)	401·3 (26·2)	1,534·2 (100·0)	2·2
Metal manufactures	475·8 (18·9)	1,377·0 (54·6)	193·2 (7·7)	40·6 (2·7)	—	3·0 (0·1)	145·2 (5·8)	288·8 (9·3)	2,523·6 (100·0)	3·6
Mining, construction industrial machinery	906·0 (40·2)	934·8 (41·5)	158·4 (7·0)	28·1 (1·2)	—	7·2 (0·3)	12·0 (0·5)	206·5 (9·3)	2,253·0 (100·0)	3·2
Electrical machinery and appliances	988·8 (26·9)	1,671·0 (45·5)	322·8 (8·8)	12·2 (0·3)	—	1·2 (—)	25·8 (0·7)	649·0 (17·8)	3,670·8 (100·0)	5·3
Road motor vehicles	103·2 (2·9)	2,653·8 (74·6)	374·4 (10·5)	0·6 (—)	—	—	—	426·6 (12·0)	3,558·6 (100·0)	5·1
Manufactured articles	497·4 (32·8)	468·6 (30·9)	187·2 (12·4)	15·6 (1·0)	—	1·2 (0·1)	19·2 (1·3)	326·4 (21·5)	1,515·6 (100·0)	2·2
Paper and paper products	333·9 (20·5)	489·4 (30·3)	147·8 (9·1)	96·3 (6·0)	—	0·9 (—)	160·1 (9·9)	389·2 (24·1)	1,617·4 (100·0)	2·3
Other	5,167·7 (15·4)	11,265·7 (33·7)	2,325·6 (7·0)	903·9 (2·7)	449·4 (1·3)	1,158·0 (3·5)	3,733·9 (11·2)	8,457·4 (25·2)	33,461·6 (100·0)	18·0
TOTAL IMPORTS	11,040·6 (15·8)	20,667·6 (00·0)	5,398·8 (00·0)	1,557·3 (2·2)	449·4 (0·6)	7,342·8 (10·5)	7,093·2 (10·2)	16,171·5 (23·4)	69,721·2 (100·0)	100·0

Source: Worksheets of a study prepared by F. Andic and S. Andic for the Caribbean Development Project of the Twentieth Century Fund.

Notes
1. BW $1.00 = US $0.60.
2. Bracketed figures indicate percentages of total imports.
3. EFTA excludes UK, shown separately.

Table 4 Barbados. Geographical destination of major exports, 1965
(US $000)

	USA	UK	EEC	EFTA	CACM	LAFTA	CARIFTA	Other	Total xs	% Distribution by Commodity
Molasses	889·8 (38·3)	43·2 (1·9)	—	—	—	—	3·6 (0·2)	1,389·0 (59·6)	2,325·6 (100·0)	(8·1)
Sugar	830·4 (4·2)	15,649·2 (78·7)	—	—	—	—	41·4 (0·2)	3,352·8 (16·9)	19,873·8 (100·0)	(69·6)
Crustacea and molluscs	1,913·4 (99·1)	—	—	—	—	—	12·0 (0·6)	5·4 (0·3)	1,930·8 (100·0)	(6·8)
Lard, margarine	—	—	—	0·6 (—)	—	—	579·6 (100·0)	—	579·6 (100·0)	(2·0)
Rum	18·6 (1·1)	112·8 (6·9)	21·6 (1·3)	—	—	—	769·2 (47·2)	707·4 (43·5)	1,630·2 (100·0)	(5·7)
Other	120·6 (5·4)	287·4 (12·9)	75·0 (3·4)	—	—	4·8 (0·2)	1,415·4 (63·4)	327·0 (14·7)	2,230·2 (100·0)	(7·8)
TOTAL EXPORTS	3,772·8 (13·2)	16,092·6 (56·3)	96·6 (0·3)	0·6 (—)	—	4·8 (0·2)	2,821·2 (9·9)	5,781·6 (20·2)	28,570·2 (100·0)	(100·0)

Source: Worksheets of a study prepared by F. Andic and S. Andic for the Caribbean Development Project of the Twentieth Century Fund.
Notes
1. BW $1.00 = US $0.60.
2. Bracketed figures indicate percentage of total exports.
3. EFTA excludes UK, shown separately.

Table 5 Dominican Republic. Geographical origin of major import commodities, 1966
(US $000)

	USA	EEC	EFTA	CACM	LAFTA	CARIFTA	Other	Total imports	% Distribution by commodity
Chemical and pharmaceutical	5,051 (48·0)	2,237 (21·2)	1,095 (10·4)	1 (—)	425 (4·0)	13 (0·1)	1,707 (16·3)	10,529 (100·0)	(6·5)
Machinery and apparatus	5,389 (54·4)	1,545 (15·6)	876 (8·8)	2 (—)	228 (2·3)	60 (0·6)	1,812 (18·3)	9,912 (100·0)	(6·2)
Motor vehicles	6,614 (48·4)	2,463 (18·0)	2,359 (17·4)	4 (—)	37 (0·3)	3 (—)	2,176 (15·9)	13,676 (100·0)	(8·5)
Iron and steel and manufactures	4,301 (40·1)	3,490 (32·5)	966 (9·0)	—	17 (0·2)	2 (—)	1,961 (18·3)	10,737 (100·0)	(6·7)
Electrical equipment	4,658 (61·3)	834 (11·0)	228 (3·0)	—	21 (0·3)	...	1,863 (24·5)	7,604 (100·0)	(4·7)
Cotton fabrics	2,600 (43·4)	145 (2·4)	90 (1·5)	...	...	—	3,159 (52·7)	5,994 (100·0)	(3·7)
Milk	1,630 (33·2)	3,049 (62·1)	214 (4·4)	—	—	—	16 (0·3)	4,909 (100·0)	(3·1)
Wheat and wheat flour	5,144 (100·0)	—	—	—	—	—	—	5,144 (100·0)	(3·2)
Gasoline	—	—	—	—	—	2,760 (45·2)	3,351 (54·8)	6,111 (100·0)	(3·8)
Paper and paper manufactures	4,332 (60·7)	1,036 (14·5)	560 (7·8)	—	34 (0·5)	2 (—)	1,170 (16·4)	7,134 (100·0)	(4·4)
Rubber and rubber manufactures	1,562 (33·1)	839 (17·8)	419 (8·9)	—	2 (—)	—	1,900 (40·2)	4,722 (100·0)	(2·9)
Crude oil for fuel	—	—	—	—	1,906 (44·9)	354 (8·3)	1,983 (46·7)	4,243 (100·0)	(2·6)
Fish: dried, salted	22 (0·6)	133 (3·7)	2,412 (67·8)	—	—	—	989 (27·8)	3,556 (100·0)	(2·2)
Iron and steel: construction materials	724 (17·1)	2,089 (49·3)	84 (2·0)	—	—	2 (—)	1,335 (31·5)	4,234 (100·0)	(2·6)
Other	32,152 (51·7)	8,297 (13·3)	3,658 (5·9)	11 (—)	627 (1·0)	746 (1·2)	16,757 (26·9)	62,248 (100·0)	(38·7)
TOTAL IMPORTS	74,179 (46·1)	26,157 (16·3)	12,981 (8·1)	18 (—)	3,297 (2·1)	3,942 (2·4)	40,179 (25·0)	160,753 (100·0)	(100·0)

Source: Worksheets of a study prepared by F. Andic and S. Andic for the Caribbean Development Project of the Twentieth Century Fund.
1. US $1.00 = DR $1.00.
2. Bracketed figures indicate percentages of total imports.
3. CARIFTA includes only Barbados, Guyana, Jamaica, Trinidad and Tobago.

Table 6 Dominican Republic. Geographical direction of major export commodities, 1966
(US $000)

	USA	EEC	EFTA	CACM	LAFTA	CARIFTA	Other	Total xs	% Distribution by commodity
Bauxite	10,246 (99·0)	—	—	—	—	100 (1·0)	—	10,346 (100·0)	(7·6)
Sugar and its derivatives	76,134 (99·2)	—	—	—	—	—	606 (0·8)	76,740 (100·0)	(56·1)
Cocoa and its derivatives	11,081 (98·9)	—	—	—	—	—	118 (1·1)	11,199 (100·0)	(8·2)
Tobacco and its derivatives	591 (8·9)	3,343 (50·3)	48 (0·7)	—	—	—	2,657 (40·1)	6,642 (100·0)	(4·9)
Banana	225 (29·6)	447 (58·9)	23 (3·0)	—	—	—	64 (8·4)	759 (100·0)	(0·6)
Coffee	16,027 (76·5)	4,129 (19·7)	216 (1·0)	—	—	—	578 (2·8)	20,950 (100·0)	(15·3)
Other	4,893 (48·5)	668 (6·6)	1,453 (14·4)	62 (0·6)	400 (4·0)	38 (0·4)	2,566 (25·5)	10,080 (100·0)	(7·4)
TOTAL EXPORTS	119,197 (87·2)	8,587 (6·3)	1,740 (1·3)	62 (0·6)	403 (0·3)	138 (0·1)	6,589 (4·8)	136,716 (100·0)	(100·0)

Source: Worksheets of a study prepared by F. Andic and S. Andic for the Caribbean Development Project of the Twentieth Century Fund.
Notes
1. US $1.00 = DR $1.00.
2. Bracketed figures indicate percentages of total exports.
3. CARIFTA includes only Barbados, Guyana, Jamaica, Trinidad and Tobago.

Table 7 Jamaica. Geographical origin of major imports, 1965
(US $000)

	USA	UK	EEC	EFTA	CACM	LAFTA	CARIFTA	Other	Total imports	% Distribution by commodity
Rice	4,272·8 (61·2)	—	106·4 (1·5)	—	—	—	2,604·0 (37·3)	—	6,986·0 (100·0)	2·4
Flour	2,371·6 (24·8)	—	2,774·8 (29·0)	—	—	—	—	4,410·0 (46·2)	9,556·4 (100·0)	3·2
Petroleum and products	2,601·2 (5·5)	254·8 (0·5)	75·6 (0·2)	2·8 (—)	—	22,111·6 (46·7)	142·8 (0·3)	22,195·6 (46·8)	47,384·4 (100·0)	16·1
Miscellaneous chemical materials	3,192·0 (50·9)	1,422·4 (22·7)	599·2 (9·5)	212·8 (3·4)	...	8·4 (0·1)	5·6 (0·1)	834·4 (13·3)	6,274·8 (100·0)	2·1
Paper and paperboard	3,105·2 (42·6)	898·8 (12·3)	100·8 (1·4)	985·6 (13·5)	—	—	—	2,200·8 (30·2)	7,291·2 (100·0)	2·5
Textile fabrics of standard type	1,890·2 (28·5)	1,638·0 (24·7)	72·8 (1·1)	36·4 (0·5)	—	—	—	2,984·8 (45·2)	6,622·0 (100·0)	2·3
Iron and steel	2,032·8 (14·4)	5,885·6 (40·0)	4,401·6 (29·9)	274·4 (1·9)	—	—	—	2,122·4 (13·8)	14,716·8 (100·0)	5·0
Manufactures of metal	3,264·8 (32·3)	4,034·8 (39·9)	988·4 (9·8)	128·8 (1·3)	—	25·2 (0·2)	19·6 (0·2)	1,654·8 (16·3)	10,116·4 (100·0)	3·4
Machinery; mining and construction	11,216·8 (57·9)	5,437·6 (28·1)	1,327·2 (6·9)	302·4 (1·6)	—	56·0 (0·3)	...	1,027·6 (5·2)	19,367·6 (100·0)	6·6
Electric machinery	4,082·4 (34·9)	4,522·0 (38·7)	1,262·8 (10·8)	106·4 (0·9)	8·4 (0·1)	2·8 (—)	...	1,702·4 (14·6)	11,687·2 (100·0)	4·0
Road motor vehicles	1,615·6 (7·3)	1,551·2 (7·0)	1,122·8 (5·1)	36·4 (0·2)	—	—	...	17,810·8 (80·4)	22,136·8 (100·0)	7·5
Manufactured articles	2,903·6 (41·9)	1,778·0 (25·7)	470·4 (6·8)	473·2 (6·8)	—	2·8 (—)	...	1,299·2 (19·0)	6,927·2 (100·0)	2·4
Other	48,174·0 (38·5)	43,442·0 (34·8)	11,202·8 (9·0)	3,768·8 (3·0)	3,771·6 (3·0)	898·8 (0·7)	1,940·4 (1·6)	11,810·4 (9·4)	125,008·8 (100·0)	<2·5
TOTAL IMPORTS	90,725·6 (30·9)	70,865·2 (24·1)	24,505·6 (8·3)	6,330·8 (2·2)	3,780·0 (1·3)	23,102·8 (7·9)	4,718·0 (1·6)	70,050·4 (23·7)	294,078·4 (100.0)	100·0

Source: Worksheets of a study prepared by F. Andic and S. Andic for the Caribbean Development Project of the Twentieth Century Fund.
Notes
1. US $2.8 = £1.00.
2. Bracketed figures indicate percentage of total imports.
3. EFTA excludes UK, shown separately.

Table 8   Jamaica. Geographical direction of major exports, 1965
(US $000)

	USA	UK	EFTA	EEC	CACM	LAFTA	CARIFTA	Other	Total xs	% Distribution by commodity
Alumina	4,550·0 (9·3)	—	18,866·4 (38·5)	—	—	—	8·4 (—)	25,555·6 (52·2)	48,980·4 (100·0)	(23·3)
Bauxite	49,865·2 (100·0)	—	—	—	—	—	—	—	49,865·2 (100·0)	(23·7)
Bananas	—	16,354·8 (95·7)	—	733·4 (4·3)	—	—	—	—	17,091·2 (100·0)	(8·1)
Fruit and juices	266·0 (3·3)	6,112·4 (75·8)	11·2 (0·1)	733·6 (9·1)	—	—	207·2 (2·6)	736·4 (9·1)	8,066·8 (100·0)	(3·8)
Coffee	2·8 (0·4)	344·4 (46·9)	50·4 (6·9)	42·0 (5·7)	—	—	2·8 (0·4)	291·2 (39·7)	733·6 (100·0)	(0·3)
Pimento	361·2 (14·3)	154·0 (6·1)	249·2 (9·9)	1,041·6 (41·3)	—	...	...	714·0 (28·4)	2,520·0 (100·0)	(1·2)
Rum	2,335·2 (52·9)	971·6 (22·0)	249·2 (5·6)	347·2 (7·9)	—	...	...	512·4 (11·6)	4,415·6 (100·0)	(2·1)
Sugar	9,354·8 (21·4)	27,969·2 (63·9)	—	—	—	—	—	6,434·4 (14·7)	43,758·4 (100·0)	(20·8)
Other	13,361·6 (38·5)	5,779·2 (16·7)	53·2 (0·1)	946·4 (2·7)	1,464·4 (4·2)	218·4 (0·6)	2,500·4 (7·8)	10,362·8 (29·4)	34,686·4 (100·0)	(16·5)
TOTAL EXPORTS	80,096·8 (38·1)	57,680·0 (27·5)	19,476·8 (9·3)	3,844·4 (1·8)	1,464·4 (0·7)	218·4 (0·1)	2,721·6 (1·3)	44,618·0 (21·2)	210,120·4 (100·0)	(100·0)

Source: Worksheets of a study prepared by F. Andic and S. Andic for the Caribbean Development Project of the Twentieth Century Fund.

Notes
1. US **$2.8** = £1.00.
2. Bracketed figures indicate percentages of total exports.
3. EFTA excludes UK, shown separately.

Table 9 Surinam. Geographical origin of major import commodity groups, 1965 (us $000)

	USA	EEC	EFTA	CACM	LAFTA	CARIFTA	Other	Total	% Distribution by commodity group
Flour	1,288·9 (78·6)	192·6 (11·7)	—	—	0·5 (—)	7·4 (0·5)	151·3 (9·2)	1,640·7 (100·0)	1·7
Meat and meat preparations	761·4 (61·9)	299·5 (24·3)	78·8 (6·4)	—	9·5 (0·8)	16·9 (1·4)	64·9 (5·2)	1,230·7 (100·0)	1·3
Beverage and tobacco	321·2 (22·2)	815·3 (56·4)	285·2 (19·7)	—	—	10·6 (0·7)	14·3 (1·0)	1,446·6 (100·0)	1·5
Petroleum and petroleum products	314·8 (5·2)	59·3 (1·0)	55·6 (0·9)	—	—	5,434·4 (89·9)	178·3 (3·0)	6,042·3 (100·0)	6·4
Rubber and rubber products	697·3 (38·7)	541·8 (30·1)	348·1 (19·3)	—	37·6 (2·1)	9·5 (0·5)	166·2 (9·3)	1,800·5 (100·0)	1·9
Paper and paper products	337·6 (14·3)	1,019·5 (43·3)	73·5 (3·1)	—	—	30·2 (1·3)	894·7 (38·0)	2,355·6 (100·0)	2·5
Textiles, yarns, wastes	1,194·7 (34·0)	538·1 (15·3)	133·9 (3·8)	—	—	83·6 (2·4)	1,561·3 (44·5)	3,511·6 (100·0)	3·7
Iron and steel manufacturers	7,837·0 (58·0)	3,603·7 (26·6)	423·8 (3·1)	—	6·9 (0·1)	48·7 (0·4)	1,602·6 (11·8)	13,522·7 (100·0)	14·2
Machinery	9,311·1 (66·9)	2,794·1 (20·1)	1,407·9 (10·1)	—	33·9 (0·2)	25·4 (12·6)	353·5 (2·5)	13,925·9 (100·0)	14·7
Electrical machinery and appliances	2,961·4 (48·0)	2,374·1 (38·6)	413·8 (6·7)	—	2·1 (—)	15·9 (0·3)	377·7 (6·4)	6,145·0 (100·0)	6·5
Motor vehicles and parts	2,252·4 (34·9)	2,510·0 (39·1)	1,362·4 (21·1)	—	—	23·3 (0·4)	307·4 (4·5)	6,455·5 (100·0)	6·8
Other	16,999·5 (46·1)	11,816·4 (32·0)	2,623·3 (7·1)	6·3 (—)	974·1 (2·6)	669·8 (1·8)	3,809·0 (10·4)	36,898·4 (100·0)	18·8
TOTAL IMPORTS	44,277·3 (46·6)	26,564·4 (28·0)	7,206·3 (7·6)	6·3 (—)	1,064·6 (1·1)	6,375·7 (6·6)	9,480·9 (10·3)	94,975·5 (100·0)	(100·0)

Source: Worksheets of a study prepared by F. Andic and S. Andic for the Caribbean Development Project of the Twentieth Century Fund.

Notes
1. us $1.00= Sf 1.89.
2. Bracketed figures indicate percentages of total imports.
3. Of total eec imports, 72 per cent come from the Netherlands.

Table 10 Surinam. Geographical direction of major export commodities, 1965
(US $000)

	USA	EEC	EFTA	CACM	LAFTA	CARIFTA	Other	Total	% Distribution by commodity
Bauxite	40,445.5 (88.0)	90.5 (0.2)	—	—	37.0 (0.1)	—	5,366.1 (11.7)	45,939.1 (100.0)	(79.7)
Timber	282.5 (9.1)	557.1 (17.9)	9.0 (0.3)	—	—	338.6 (10.9)	1,924.5 (61.8)	3,111.7 (100.0)	(5.4)
Rice	—	2,184.7 (85.0)	59.8 (2.3)	—	—	139.1 (5.4)	187.8 (7.3)	2,571.4 (100.0)	(4.5)
Paper and paper products	12.7 (1.3)	619.0 (63.2)	66.1 (6.7)	—	—	160.1 (16.4)	121.8 (12.4)	979.9 (100.0)	(1.7)
Fish and fish preparations	689.4 (54.6)	5.3 (0.4)	—	—	—	—	568.8 (45.0)	1,263.5 (100.0)	(2.2)
Citrus	—	388.9 (94.0)	—	—	—	0.5 (0.1)	24.4 (5.9)	413.8 (100.0)	(0.7)
Textiles	—	75.7 (20.3)	—	—	0.5 (0.1)	43.4 (11.6)	253.4 (68.0)	373.0 (100.0)	(0.6)
Coffee	18.5 (11.9)	129.1 (83.0)	7.9 (5.1)	—	—	—	—	155.5 (100.0)	(0.3)
Cocoa	—	107.9 (95.8)	—	—	—	—	4.8 (4.2)	112.7 (100.0)	(0.2)
Banana and plantains	—	572.5 (100.0)	—	—	—	—	—	572.5 (100.0)	(1.0)
Other	767.7 (35.5)	1,180.4 (54.5)	16.4 (0.8)	—	0.5 (—)	22.7 (1.1)	177.9 (8.1)	2,165.6 (100.0)	(3.7)
TOTAL EXPORTS	42,216.4 (73.2)	5,910.6 (10.3)	159.3 (0.3)	—	38.1 (0.1)	704.8 (1.3)	8,629.5 (14.8)	57,658.7 (100.0)	(100.0)

Source: Calculated from worksheets of a study prepared by F. Andic and S. Andic for the Caribbean Development Project of the Twentieth Century Fund.

Notes
1. US $1.00 = Sf 1.89.
2. Bracketed figures indicate percentages of total exports.
3. Of shipments to EEC, 75 per cent goes to the Netherlands.

Chapter 4

INTEGRATION MOVEMENTS IN THE CARIBBEAN

In the developed, as well as the developing, world, the desire for economic integration, whatever the factors which give rise to it, has been so well crystallized that from the iron curtain countries to Western Europe, from East Africa to Latin America structurally homogeneous or heterogeneous countries have made efforts to form integrated blocs and have already coined the slogan referring to the mid-twentieth century as the 'age of integration'.

Theoretically, possibilities of forming integrated economic blocks are as many as the number of existing blocs. In reality the alternatives are limited by political, economic, and geographic factors. For any one of our five countries the choice cannot extend beyond three alternatives. First and foremost there already is in the Caribbean an indigenous movement of integration (Caribbean Free Trade Association—CARIFTA). Then, in the geographical proximity of the region there is first of all the Central American Common Market (CACM) consisting of five fairly similar small economies; and secondly the Latin American Free Trade Association (LAFTA), though geographically large, is, economically, only potentially great, and yet to be put on a sound and well-functioning foundation. Finally there is the seemingly distant European Economic Community (EEC), well-established, functioning relatively smoothly since 1957, and by far the most successful of all integration movements. For political reasons, rather than economic, it has acquired already a few associate members in the Caribbean, and might acquire a few more, especially if Great Britain becomes the seventh member.

76

With varying degrees of relevance these four would constitute the real alternatives for our five countries, not only because of their direct interest in these blocs, but also because of the interest, direct and/or tangential, of the blocs themselves, specifically CARIFTA and EEC, in our five economies. Consequently the present chapter provides a descriptive and analytical study of the economic blocs concerned. This information, together with the trade patterns in major import and export commodity groups, will lead to the choice of the alternatives for any one of the five countries, on which the work of Part III will be based.

I. The Central American Common Market

1. CREATION AND MEMBERSHIP

Five Central American countries—Costa Rica, El Salvador, Guatemala, Honduras, and Nicaragua—form the regional economic organization known as the Central American Common Market. Altogether they have a population estimated in 1967 to be approximately 14 million and a gross domestic product of $4·3 billion. Disparities between the five economies are not excessive: per capita gross output ranges from $250 in Honduras to $430 in Costa Rica, which also has the smallest population.

CACM is the culmination of sustained efforts involving a series of treaty actions beginning in 1950. The first integration agreement—The Multilateral Free Trade Treaty—was signed in 1958 stipulating the creation of a customs union over a period of ten years, and a regime of Central American integration industries. This was replaced in 1960 by the General Treaty of Central American Integration, or the Managua Treaty. Guatemala, El Salvador, and Nicaragua signed the Treaty in 1960; Costa Rica in 1962. The Treaty became effective in June 1961 for Guatemala, El Salvador and Nicaragua; in April 1962 for Honduras; and in September 1963 for Costa Rica.

CACM does not have a definite policy with respect to the entry of members, other than the present five, into the Common Market. In fact one of the objectives of the Treaty of Managua is the preservation of the internal unity of the region. This is expressed in Article XXV which stipulates that no member country can multilaterally sign treaties and/or agreements with countries outside of Central American economic integration. Thus the 'Central American Exception Clause' (Cláusula Centroamericana de Excepción) supersedes the most-favoured-nation treatment which members may enjoy in their commercial relations with non-members.

Table 11 CACM. Population and GDP, 1967

	Population (million)	%	GDP (US $ million)	%	Per capita GDP ($)
Costa Rica	1·6	11·7	692	16·2	432
El Salvador	3·2	23·4	890	20·8	278
Guatemala	4·7	34·3	1,445	33·7	307
Honduras	2·4	17·5	596	13·9	248
Nicaragua	1·8	13·1	660	15·4	367
Total	13·7	100·0	4,283	100·0	

Rates of Exchange: Costa Rica $1.00 = C6.62
El Salvador $1.00 = C2.50
Guatemala $1.00 = Q1.00
Honduras $1.00 = L2.00
Nicaragua $1.00 = Cór. 7.00

Source: Compiled from information given in IMF, *International Financial Statistics* XXII, 4 (1969).

Nevertheless negotiations are being made with Panama, with LAFTA, and with the Dominican Republic, in order to find ways in which the CACM can be expanded to include these additional areas, especially since it is presently confronted with a balance of payments crisis with respect to the rest of the world and is looking for means by which to increase extra-regional exports in face of galloping imports.

Negotiations for Panama's entry began in 1963; after various studies by the Permanent Secretariat of the CACM (SIECA— Secretaría Permanente del Tratado General de Integración Económica Centroamericana)[1] and by the Government of Panama,[2] and participation by Panama in the activities of

[1] SIECA, *La participación de Panamá en el programa de integración económica centroamericana*, Guatemala, March 1967.

[2] Ramón Tamames, *Aspectos económicos de la vinculación de Panamá al Mercado Común Centroamericano*, Panamá: Ministerio de Relaciones Exteriores, Departamento de Comercio Internacional, 1966.

various subsidiary organisms of the CACM, the entry of this country, even as an associate member, is still a remote possibility.

A study was proposed as early as 1966 on the possibility of co-operation between the CACM and LAFTA. Such a co-operation found its support in the Declaration of the Presidents of America (Punta del Este, Uruguay, April 14, 1967), and at the San Salvador meeting of the Presidents of Central America in July 1968 in the expressed desire for the formation of a co-ordinating commission between LAFTA and CACM with the aim of eventual achievement of a Latin American Common Market.[3] Nevertheless serious steps are not being taken by the CACM, since neither exports to Latin America are significant (1·4 per cent of total exports in 1967) nor are export possibilities to Latin America considered to be all that promising. *Prima facie* there may appear to be a potential advantage for CACM to associate within LAFTA with petroleum producing members, i.e. Venezuela, from which crude petroleum is imported. But, as shall be seen subsequently, oil products are extremely delicate to handle in the negotiations within the CACM, and would probably cause more headaches than cures for strengthening the industrial base—because of the difficulty of overriding specific vested interests—unless oil refining activities can be efficiently combined with exports to the rest of the world.

The Dominican Republic has been sounding for some time the possibility of entry, in one form or another, with the support of international financial institutions, such as the Inter-American Development Bank,[4] and has made efforts to define its position *vis-à-vis* the Central American process of integration. Such an entry, if at all, will come only after long negotiations which will probably first allow small-scale liberalization of

[3] In 1967 Mexico had requested from LAFTA that the free trade area grant concessions to CACM members, and a decision was signed by all members. It was, however, never implemented, since the relatively less developed members, especially Ecuador, were not keen on having competition with their products, such as cocoa and banana, which CACM also produces and exports.

[4] Ramón Tamames, *Las alternativas de la República Dominicana frente a la integración económica en Latinoamérica*, Buenos Aires: Instituto de Integración de América Latina (INTAL), 1967.

trade between the two economic units, ultimately leading to integration

Currently there are two trends of thought at the CACM head-quarters with respect to admitting future members. One is the realization of the bitter fact that the aggregate market size of the CACM, as it is, is too small to ensure accelerated economic growth, and that industrialization requires the expansion of exports beyond the Central American region. Hence acceptance of the idea of possible integration with other economic units. The second line of thought stresses the significant role of political factors, which find their *raison d'être* in the history of the area, which shall not be entered into. It maintains that the ultimate aim of the CACM is to achieve political unity, and admission of other members would hinder this achievement. Hence the rejection of effective integration with other areas. The developments in Central America suggest that the first line of thought will overpower the second.

It should also be noted that the Treaty, as it is, does not provide for any institution, like the Commission of the EEC, which would have the power to study and act upon this matter.

2. OBJECTIVES

The general objective of the Central American integration movemetn, as is so often repeated in integration theory as well as during the processes of actual formation of integrated blocs among the less-developed countries, is a vigorous change in the traditional structure of the economies concerned. It is maintained that only through diversification of the economic structure away from the preponderance of the agricultural sector towards gradual industrialization can:

(a) economic and social progress be accelerated;
(b) viability of a sustained and balanced economic and social development be assured;
(c) the economic and social structure be modernized;
(d) higher standards of living be ensured;
(e) the economic ties be strengthened with a world which tends more and more towards the formation of blocs in continental dimensions.

There is, therefore, a great stress on the preference for the development of regional/domestic industries protected from the competitive external world, in other words on the creation of import-competing industries. The need for such industrialization arises from the fact that none of the member economies is complementary with any other; all have been oriented to the production and export of similar traditional agricultural primary products of banana, coffee, cocoa, cotton, sugar, timber, meat, and sesame seeds. In 1967, for example, the ratio of the value of such exports to the total exports to developed countries was still 87 per cent for the region as a whole.[5] In addition the size of the individual markets is too small for industrialization even on a moderate scale. The fact that intra-regional trade has grown from a mere 6 per cent of total external trade in 1960 to about one-fourth in 1967 and that the major share of this trade is represented by manufactured articles is indicative of the intra-zonal trade expansion of manufactured products as is expected from a strict policy of import substitution accompanied by trade liberalization, of the area's high preference for industrialization, and of the potential complementarity between the members.

But industrialization is not equivalent to import substitution; it should also incorporate export-oriented industries if the balance of payments position is to improve, if not worsen, and if a structural change is to take place in total trade production instead of only within the region. There is serious concern at the CACM headquarters over the rising trade deficit with the rest of the world. Because of booming exports, this deficit was not very significant at the end of the fifties, but it doubled between 1963 and 1965 and again between 1965 and 1967, soaring to $284 million in the latter year.[6] The reason for the tremendous increase in the deficit in the external account was the stagnation of exports —precisely because they consisted largely of primary agricultural products—coupled with an 11 per cent increase in imports

[5] Computed from data given in IMF, *International Financial Statistics*, XXII: 5, May 1969, and *idem.*, *Direction of Trade, Annual 1963–67*.

[6] See ECLA, 'Informe de la Secretaría del Comité de Cooperación Económica sobre el Mercado Común Centroamericano 1966–1968', CEPAL/MEX/69/1, January 17, 1969 (mimeo).

F

both in 1966 and 1967—precisely because of the dependence of import competing industries, so prominent in intra-zonal trade, on imported intermediate products. Consequently, the CACM has now come to realize that regional industrialization alone is not sufficient if economic diversification is to take place on a comprehensive scale, but that exports will have to be diversified as well. In other words, it is not enough to save foreign exchange, but it is absolutely essential to earn it as well. Given the traditional character of the economies concerned, the next objective of the CACM will then be the promotion of export-oriented manufacturing industries to increase foreign exchange earning. Promotional work in this direction has already started. It is expected that industries utilising regionally available raw materials, such as forestry products and certain minerals, can be set up and that this would lead to a whole chain of forward linkages of manufactured products.

Undoubtedly the CACM is also concerned with the assurance of balanced distribution of the benefits and costs of regional trading and industrialization arrangements or at least with preventing some members from gaining at the expense of others. This idea runs through almost every statement dealing with the integration movement. The practical solution to this aspect of integration calls for the co-ordination of the policies in the individual spheres of trade, investments, industry, agriculture, mining, infrastructure, and technical and financial assistance.

To summarize, the objectives of the CACM are:

(a) a high rate of economic growth;

(b) a high preference for industry;

(c) broadening the export base;

(d) reducing the deficit in the balance of payments;

(e) equitable distribution of the gains and losses;

(f) implicit in all the above objectives, mobilization of unemployed resources.

3. ECONOMIC POLICY INSTRUMENTS

The Multilateral Free Trade Treaty of 1958 stipulated the creation of a free trade area among the five members and agreed on a regime for integration of industries within the region. Free trade was recognized for commodities of regional origin specified in an annexed list, to be extended to all regional commodities over a period of ten years. The regime for regional integration industries had the aim of promoting new, and existing, industries. The subsequent General Treaty of Managua transformed the free trade area into a common market (Art. I) with the intermediate step of a customs union, and free trade for all commodities of regional origin, except those specified in Annex A. It is to the perfection of this customs union that the efforts of the SIECA are committed today, rather than taking active steps towards the formation of a common market. The General Treaty also endorsed the Agreement on the Regime of Integration Industries and called for protocols to specify the industries and the free trade conditions from which their products would benefit as opposed to industries designated as non-integration. It also set up the Central American Bank for Economic Integration (CABEI) '. . . to finance and promote a regionally balanced integrated economic growth . . .' (Art. XVIII), and committed the member countries '. . . to establish uniform tax incentives to industrial development . . .' (Art. XIX).

Thus the two key aspects of the Managua Treaty are the creation of a customs union with a common external tariff for commodities of regional origin, and regional industrialization to promote the economic integration and balanced economic development of the member countries. Each aspect will be taken up subsequently.

(a) *Commercial policy*

The General Treaty provides for the automatic elimination of most free trade restrictions. Nevertheless, a transition from protection to free trade cannot take place unless time is given to existing industries and economic sectors to adapt themselves to the new market conditions. Presently, therefore, there exists neither a fully liberalized intra-regional trade for products originating in the bloc, nor is there a fully established common external tariff on products originating in the rest of the world. However, great strides have been made in both directions.

With the entry of the General Treaty into effect on June 4, 1961, the intra-zonal trade of 1,028 of the total 1,276 sub-groups of commodities of the Central American Customs Nomenclature (NAUCA—Nomenclatura Arancelaria Uniforme Centroamericana) were fully liberalized. The remainder were listed in Annex A of the Treaty and were subject to prefer-ential treatment until the time when through various protocols they too would be gradually liberalized. At the end of 1968 there were only 45 subgroups which were still subject to import and export restrictions, quotas and duties for an indefinite period.[7] These mainly refer to traditional export products (coffee, cotton, sugar), products of state monopolies (rum), and articles which create special problems (wheat, wheat flour, tobacco, and oil products). All, except oil, are agricultural products and their special problems arise from the lack of other requirements, such as uniform measures governing minimum prices, financing and storage etc., without which it is impossible to establish free trade on efficient lines. The case of oil is delicate because of its production within and its large imports into the area. Guatemala, El Salvador, Costa Rica, and Nicaragua each possess oil refineries and therefore would like to protect their industries through high import levies, while Honduras levies high import duties simply for revenue purposes. In addition oil imported from the rest of the world is 98·8 per cent of total oil consumption of the region.

A common external tariff has been agreed upon on 1,504 items out of a total of 1,535. The common external tariff is put into effect through the Agreement on the Equalization of Import Duties,[8] which incorporates a list of articles on which a common

---

[7] These figures refer only to groups of commodities which move freely between *all* five members. There are, however, bilateral treaties between members which provide for the free movement of a number of commodities between them. Thus of the 45 subgroups mentioned in the text, 19 are subject to restrictions by all members, and 26 to restrictions between pairs of countries.

[8] Convenio centroamericano sobre equiparación de gravámenes a la impor-tación, San José, Costa Rica, September 1, 1959.

tariff is established immediately; the remainder are published in specific protocols. By the end of 1967 there were 31 items on which a common tariff was not determined. The major obstacle

Table 12 Overall Protection in the CACM

NAUCA Categories		Average tariff
0	Foodstuffs	14·9
1	Beverages and tobacco	60·5
2	Crude materials, excluding oil	47.9
3	Fuel oils and lubricants	45·0
4	Animal fats and vegetable oils	18·9
5	Chemical products	29·9
6	Manufactured articles	25.7
7	Machinery and transportation equipment	10.9
8	Miscellaneous manufactured articles	11.4
9	Live animals n.e.s.	15.0
	Overall average	32.4

Source: SIECA, *Arancel de Aduanas Centroamericano*, Ref. 2
Note: The table takes into consideration the following:
   (i) The immediately accepted common external tariffs.
   (ii) Progressively uniformized common external tariffs by
      (a) Convenio de equiparación (subscribed September 1, 1959)—finalized;
      (b) Protocolo de Managua (subscribed December 13, 1960)—finalized;
      (c) Protocolo de San José (subscribed July 31, 1962)—finalized;
      (d) Protocolo de Guatemala (subscribed August 1, 1964)—not yet finalized.
To these rates must be added, wherever applicable, the 30 per cent surcharge of the emergency measures arising from the balance of payments crisis.

is that despite their small number their value represents approximately 15 per cent of the total imports of the region, and therefore contributes a substantial portion of public revenues (around 25 per cent of the customs revenue of the entire region). These items are mainly motor vehicles, oil products, radio transmitting equipment, electrical equipment, wheat and wheat flour. Without an agreement on a flexible formula of the allocation of customs duties collected at the port of entry to the Treasuries of the countries to which the goods are ultimately destined, the liberalization of such products will continue to be a thorny problem.

An estimate of the protection provided by the common external tariff in various commodity subgroups is given in Table 12. The figures are obtained as a simple average of the applicable rates. The reader is reminded that qualifying enterprises benefit from exemptions from duties on machinery and equipment, raw materials, and intermediate products both within the integration scheme as well as according to national policies, such as fiscal incentive schemes, which have not yet been harmonized. Moreover in certain items the protection is even higher because of the emergency measures imposed in 1959 in face of the severe balance of payments crisis. These call for a tariff surcharge of 30 per cent on imports from the rest of the world, including imports by enterprises which enjoy fiscal exemptions within the scope of national laws and regional agreements. Certain items which are designated as essential are exempt from the surcharge.

(b) *Industrialization policy*
The industrialization policy of the CACM, as conceived by the Agreement on the Regime for Integration Industries and its two subsequent protocols, the first one of which also contains a Special System for Promotion of New Productive Activities,[9] is an illustrative example of the four criteria developed in Part I in determining the cost and benefits of specific industries to be promoted.

The Regime and the Special System each refer—implicitly—

[9] 'Convenio sobre el régimen de industrias centroamericanas de integración', Tegucigalpa, June 10, 1958; 'Protocolo al convenio sobre el régimen de industrias centroamericanas de integración', San Salvador, January 29, 1963; 'Protocolo al convenio sobre el régimen de industrias centroamericanas de integración', San Salvador, November 5, 1965; all in SIECA, *Convenios centroamericanos de integración económica*, Guatemala, Vols I and II, 1963; Vol. IV, 1968.

to different types of industries, as shall be seen subsequently. Both, however, are concerned with eliminating the lack of complementarity between the five members, and therefore aim at encouraging those industrial activities which will create complementarity. Both take into account not only the potential effect of industrialization on income, employment, and intra-zonal trade, but also emphasize the high prestige attached to the industrialization process in any developing country. The Regime is especially concerned with the avoidance of the pro-liferation of small-scale and high-cost industries so as not to drain the resources in short supply, and favours product specialization and relatively large-scale plants in order to break away from the industrialization pattern of light industries and to attract ancillary activities. The Special System, on the other hand, is set up more for activities for which considerations concerning plant size and location are not as decisive as under the Regime. Both are explicitly concerned with increasing foreign exchange savings. The only exception perhaps is the concept of income foregone, since the emphasis of the indus-trialization policy is on diversification and economic growth, and it is implicitly assumed that economic growth under protection will more than compensate for the income foregone through trade diversion.

The Regime, among other advantages, guarantees free access to the common market to the products of the 'integration industries' and provides a uniform tariff protection. To benefit from the advantages of the Regime an industrial activity will have to fulfil the following criteria:

(i) The industry can be, but need not be, new to the region. In reality, however, all industries so far encompassed by the Regime are new industries.

(ii) The new plant to be established or the activity to be expanded must require free access to the entire regional market in order to operate under reasonable economic and competitive conditions, even at minimum capacity, or in order to make effective use of its existing capacity. Thus the eligible industry can support only one firm under economically efficient condi-tions.

(iii) The operations of the industrial plant must lead to a net expansion in intra-zonal trade.

(iv) The plant must accelerate the process of industrialization by promoting the rational utilization of available capital and natural resources, improving technical skills, and, most important, by increasing foreign exchange savings. The rational utilization of developmental resources is corollary to the second condition, the increase in foreign exchange savings to the third.

(v) The location of the plant must ensure a relatively equitable distribution of industrial development throughout the region. This is ensured by the agreement that a second plant will not be awarded to any country until all the five members have been assigned a plant in conformity with the protocol. The location need not necessarily be optimal, provided that the operation is technically and economically viable. In reality, the Regime cannot prevent the uneven distribution of industries, because by definition it is applicable to a limited number of industries and even within these allows for the establishment of firms which need not request the 'integration' status.

Once the 'integration' status is bestowed upon it, the industry benefits from the following advantages:

(i) Immediate free access to the Central American market. Similar products of plants remaining outside the Regime do not have immediate free access to the regional market even though they are indigenous to the region. The duties levied on them, however, are to be reduced at a straight line rate within ten years, by which time products of both operations would move freely among the members.

(ii) Sufficient external tariff protection to make their products competitive with those of foreign producers,[10] and priority as suppliers to the governments.

(iii) Exemption from import duties and production and sales

[10] Articles 18 and 26 of the first Protocol to the Regime, and Article 10 of the second specify the common external tariff rates on imports of products similar to caustic soda and insecticides, tyres and tubes, laminated and sheet glass respectively. These are the three operations which have been designated as integration industries, the first located in Nicaragua, the second in Guatemala, and the third in Honduras.

taxes for ten years on raw materials and intermediate products used by the integration industry; exemption from quantitative restrictions on imports and currency controls.

The Special System for the Promotion of Productive Activities is accounted for in Part IV of the First Protocol to the Regime. It is a regional industrial promotion mechanism which provides for periodical joint elaboration of a list of regional manufactures which are to be granted special tariff protection, in the form of import duties higher than those specified for similar products in the common external tariff, provided that the said products were not being produced previously in any one of the five members and that installed capacity is at least 50 per cent of the regional demand. The portion of the demand not met out of regional production is to be met out of imports levied at rates no higher than those of the common external tariff. The benefits provided by the Regime to integration industries are not applicable to those which fall into the scope of the Special System and vice-versa.

The industrialization policy sketched above has so far not succeeded in being the promoting force that it was expected to be. Industrialization patterns have hardly changed since 1958.[11] Many reasons account for this failure: shortage of technical skills, scepticism of foreign investors, non-existence of a private regional capital market, relative scarcity of natural resources, etc.; reasons all too familiar to economists interested in underdevelopment. But perhaps the most important factor in this respect is that the five members have not been able to arrive at a working consensus for the application of the Regime. The Regime is an experimental exercise; no other similar system exists elsewhere. It ascribes a passive role to the Common Market authorities in designating 'integration' industries; it does not relate the concept of 'integration' industries to the global industrialization need of the area; industrial planning on a national and regional scale does not exist; and

[11] In 1962 light consumer industries accounted for 85 per cent of total manufacturing output, while in 1964 their share had declined only to 82 per cent. See Inter-American Development Bank, INTAL, *La Integración económica de América Latina*, Buenos Aires, 1968, 336.

there does not seem to be a clear understanding on the part of the member governments as to how the productive structure of the region would be affected by trade liberalization.[12]

The inexistence of a well-established national–regional industrial policy puts the integration industries at a disadvantageous position compared to those which are nationally promoted. Because of excessive controls of such industries, and of the facility of obtaining concessions from national governments, industries prefer the national regimes to the integrated scheme. In more cases than not this tends to defeat the purpose of integration.

All this is reflected in the inability of the Central American countries to change their industrial structure from one of light consumer industries to one of large-scale industrial complexes so as to take full advantage of the market size, as was envisaged by the Regime. Thus, strictly economic factors are not the only cause for the persistence of the traditional industrial structure, but socio-political factors are just as much to blame if not more.

II. Caribbean Free Trade Association

1. CREATION AND MEMBERSHIP

The CARIFTA Agreement, which came into effect on May 1, 1968, is the culmination of a series of efforts towards regional economic integration in the Caribbean which ineffectively started with the ill-fated West Indian Federation, went through the phase of a small nucleus of a regional bloc between Guyana, Antigua, and Barbados, and ultimately was given the blessing in the Fourth Heads of Government Conference held in Barbados in October 1967. The two most important resolutions of this Conference are the establishment of the CARIFTA to introduce free trade among the Commonwealth–Caribbean countries, subject to certain reservations, and of a Caribbean

---

[12] See Carlos M. Castillo, *Growth and Integration in Central America*, New York: Frederick A. Praeger, 1966, and Miguel S. Wionczek, 'Integración económica y distribución regional de las actividades industriales', *El Trimestre Económico*, 33:131, 1966, 483–4.

Regional Development Bank to extend loans to all signatories basically for infrastructural development and promotion of integration industries.

The membership of the CARIFTA encompasses the British Commonwealth countries. Antigua, Barbados, Guyana, and Trinidad and Tobago were initial members. Dominica, Grenada, St Kitts–Nevis–Anguilla, St Lucia, and St Vincent joined on July 1, 1968, and Jamaica and Montserrat on August 1, 1968. There are, therefore, eleven members: the four independent ones of Barbados, Guyana, Jamaica, and Trinidad and Tobago, and the seven Associate States. The latter are referred to as the less-developed members of the Association and have formed a common market among themselves called the East Caribbean Common Market (ECCM) which came into force on July 1, 1968.[13]

These eleven countries altogether have a population of approximately 4·5 million and a gross domestic product of over $2 billion. Per capita gross output ranges from $170 in St Vincent to $730 in Trinidad and Tobago as shown in Table 13.

Membership is open to any country which is not signatory to the original Agreement but it has to be approved by the Council. Members may also withdraw from the Association provided that they give twelve months' notice.

So far two countries in the region have shown interest in joining the CARIFTA: British Honduras and the Dominican Republic. The former, with the support of its Parliament, Chamber of Commerce, and local industrialists and exporters, is currently exploring suitable terms and conditions for possible entry and its implications on the economy, while at the same time looking into possibilities of membership in the CACM.*

[13] The common market provides for the elimination of customs duties and quantitative restrictions on commodity trade between the seven members, and of obstacles to the free movement of factors of production; for the establishment of a common external tariff; and for the co-ordination of economic policies for the development of agriculture, industry, and infrastructure and for the harmonization of fiscal and monetary policies. So far only a common external tariff has been agreed upon for the items included in the reserve list of the CARIFTA Agreement on which duties are to be phased out over a period of ten years. These tariffs are not yet being implemented. The main effect of this agreement is that the seven members now form a single customs area with respect to the CARIFTA.

* While the study was in print, British Honduras officially joined CARIFTA.

In April 1969 the government of the Dominican Republic effectively sought membership of the CARIFTA and the Regional Development Bank (RDB). This country's entry into the CARIFTA would almost double both the size of the population and of the present CARIFTA market. The Dominican Republic can produce the crops normally produced in the rest

Table 13   CARIFTA. Population and GDP

	Population		GDP		Per capita GDP
	(000)	(%)	($ million)	(%)	($)
Barbados (1966)	245	5·8	97·4	4·8	397
Guyana (1966)	662	15·7	215·3	10·6	320
Jamaica (1966)	1,859	44·0	907·0	44·6	484
Trinidad and Tobago (1966)	985	23·2	717·1	35·3	730
Antigua (1964)	60	1·4	15·1	0·7	242
Dominica (1964)	66	1·6	14·5	0·7	220
Grenada (1964)	94	2·2	18·0	0·9	191
Montserrat (1966)	15	0·4	3·3	0·2	224
St Kitts–Nevis– Anguilla (1964)	59	1·4	12·6	0·6	212
St Lucia (1964)	92	2·2	18·8	0·9	204
St Vincent (1964)	87	2·1	14·7	0·7	170
Total	4,224	100·0	2,033·8	100·0	484

Source: Worksheets of a study prepared by F. Andic and S. Andic for the Caribbean Development Project of the Twentieth Century Fund.

of the area; its industrial sector is growing, stimulated by heavy American private investments and official aid, especially after the disturbances of 1965. The addition of such a relatively large market and productive potential would lend strength to the CARIFTA and would meet somewhat the complaint that CARIFTA's market is too small to be of much advantage for economies of scale. However, even CACM's population of 14 million and GDP equal to that of CARIFTA and the Dominican

Republic combined has been seen to be not large enough to give rise to the propelling factors for economic and industrial development. But, again similar to the experience of CACM, the issue of political unity of the area is being raised especially by the Eastern Caribbean group, which is afraid of polarization in economic development and therefore insists on the RDB[14] as the effective condition for remaining within the Free Trade Association.[15] The entry of the Dominican Republic would face them with three instead of two—Jamaica and Trinidad and Tobago—economically strong members, and it is claimed that CARIFTA must not only have a common economic aim, but also a common political aim,[16] into the scope of which the Dominican Republic does not appear to fit because of language, cultural, and political differences. The issue of membership is currently being considered by the Council of CARIFTA.

2. OBJECTIVES

The main objective of the Agreement is to establish a free trade area in order to promote the expansion and diversification of trade in the Area of the Association under conditions of fair competition. It is expected that this expansion and diversification will encourage a balanced and progressive development of the economies concerned. To achieve this aim all barriers to movements of commodities between member countries are to be removed in such a way that the benefits of free trade will be disributed equitably within the Area.

Although not explicitly stated, it is implicit in the Agreement that the free trade area will ultimately lead to a common market. This can be observed in the regulation concerning the right of establishment and in the list of studies contemplated by the Secretariat and ECLA's Caribbean Regional Office in Trinidad and Tobago, all of which indicate the intention

[14] The Regional Development Bank was officially established in the latter part of 1969 and is now known as CARIBANK.

[15] Montserrat has openly stated that it had nothing to gain from CARIFTA, into which it had entered in the name of Caribbean solidarity, unless it could be in a position to offer reciprocal trade and find the means with which to buy goods from other members. See *The Trinidad Guardian*, Port of Spain, February 7, 1969.

[16] See the editorial, *Daily Gleaner*, Kingston, Jamaica, April 14, 1969.

of going beyond a free trade area. For instance, there is a study in process of preparation which examines the possibility of establishing a common external tariff to expand intra-Area trade and lead the way to the transformation of the Free Trade Association into a Customs Union.[17]

3. COMMERCIAL POLICY

The establishment of free trade entails the elimination of all types of barriers on the movement of goods between the member countries in which such commodities originate.

In one group of commodities the tariffs on imports into the so-called less-developed members are to be reduced over a period of ten years, the rate of duty being reduced by 50 per cent by 1973 and completely eliminated by 1978. By contrast, the tariffs on imports of the same commodities into the remaining members are to be eliminated immediately as of entry into effect of the Agreement.

In a second group of commodities the less-developed areas are again asked to reduce tariffs on imports over a period of ten years, but the remaining members are to reduce their tariffs over five years.

In a third group of commodities the distinction is made between the revenue and protective element of the import duty; the difference between the two is to be eliminated over five years, except for rum for which the less-developed members are allowed a transitional period of ten years.

There are rules of origin to determine whether a product is indigenous to the region. The destination principle is used in the taxation of goods traded between the members. Member territories agree not to levy any export duties on commodities that enter intra-Area trade and to abolish the existing ones, with the exception of those on cocoa, copra, sugar, coconut oil, nutmeg, sweet potatoes, arrowroot, peanuts, and bauxite, which will continue to be levied for the next ten years.

[17] The study is to be financed by the larger territories; the smaller territories are willing to co-operate, provided the RDB is established. Thus they expect to compensate for the revenue losses derived from accepting the common external tariff out of funds they hope to draw from the Bank.

A number of safeguard clauses are agreed upon to ensure a smooth transition from the present state to one of complete free movement of commodities and to prevent disparities in the economic and social development of the members. Tariffs levied by the less-developed members may be allowed to continue if they are considered vital for their economies. Deflection of trade is dealt with by altering some of the criteria for the determination of the origin of the product. Quantitative restrictions on imports may be allowed to continue should an appreciable rise occur in unemployment in the particular sector of industry or region in a member country, or should serious balance of payments difficulties arise from the liberalization of inter-Area trade. One specific safeguard clause protects the petroleum products of Guyana by allowing her to impose quantitative restrictions on imports of such products, and a general safeguard clause for the promotion of industrial development in less-developed territories also allows quantitative trade restrictions.

The Agreement is based essentially on the assumption of the functioning of free competition between the member countries. Consequently, no aid or subsidy to exports can be permitted, since this would entail unfair competition and distortion of trade. This rule does not apply to agricultural products until a common agricultural policy is reached; it also does not apply to manufactured products until a common incentives programme is drawn up.

Two protocols have been negotiated after the ratification of the CARIFTA Agreement. One refers to the marketing of agricultural products restricting the imports from non-member countries of agricultural commodities which are produced within the region in ample supply to satisfy the regional demand, and commits the members to buy regionally before having recourse to imports. It appears that this protocol has been specially designed to provide an expansion in the production and trade of the products of the primarily agricultural less-developed members of the Association. The Secretariat is responsible for the allocation of markets and for fixing the price of quantities exported to the region.

The second protocol refers to the marketing of unrefined sugar. It allows any member country to apply quantitative restrictions on intra-Area imports of sugar to prevent deflection of trade which could arise from the differences in the price determination practices in member countries for the sale of sugar for internal consumption, and which could lead to the movement of sugar from one sugar-producing member to another.

The Agricultural Marketing Protocol is not being implemented, because it encounters institutional difficulties: there seems to be an unwillingness to buy regionally produced goods; the implied price control is resisted; and one single government distribution centre is also resisted, especially by importers who are able to exert political pressure.

3. INDUSTRIALIZATION POLICY
CARIFTA has not yet drawn up a definite industrialization policy. Nevertheless, the ECLA Regional Office is assisting the Secretariat to help set up an industrialization scheme more or less along the lines of the integrated industries scheme of the CACM. It is carrying out studies related to: (a) the identification and establishment of industries in the less-developed members; (b) the provision of special protection for certain industries and the location of such industries; (c) setting up a regional policy of incentives to industry bearing in mind the needs of the less-developed members for preferential treatment; and (d) the feasibility of establishing certain regional industries.

III. Latin American Free Trade Association

1. CREATION AND MEMBERSHIP
LAFTA, formally agreed in February 1960 in Montevideo, Uruguay, is a free trade area between eleven members[18] with substantial differences in their income levels and their respective stages of economic development. In 1967 per capita income

---

[18] ALALC, *Tratado de Montevideo. Resoluciones Conferencia Años 1961–1967. Primera Reunión de Ministros de Relaciones Exteriores Año 1966*, Montevideo, 1968. The original signatories were Argentina, Brazil, Chile, Mexico, Paraguay, Peru, and Uruguay; Colombia and Ecuador joined in 1961, Venezuela in 1966, and Bolivia in 1967.

varied from $194 in Bolivia to $990 in Venezuela. Four countries—Argentina, Brazil, Venezuela, and Mexico—produce 80
per cent of the gross output of the Association, the remaining 20
per cent being distributed among the remaining seven again in a

Table 14 LAFTA. Population and GDP, 1967

	Population (Million)	(%)	GDP ($ million)	(%)	Per capita GDP ($)
Bolivia	3·8	1·7	735·5	0·8	194
Chile	9.1	4·2	4,838·6	5·5	532
Columbia	19·2	8·8	5,280·0	6·0	275
Ecuador	5·7	2·6	1,255·0	1·4	220
Perú	12·4	5·6	4,008·0	4·5	323
Andean Community	50·2	22·9	16,117·1	18·2	321
Venezuela	9·4	4·3	9,304·0	10·5	990
Argentina	23·3	10·6	16,348·0ª	18·5	714
Brazil	85·6	39·1	20,180·0ª	22·9	243
Mexico	45·7	20·8	24,512·0	27·8	536
Paraguay	2·2	1·0	492·3	0·6	224
Uruguay	2·8	1·3	1,355·3	1·5	484
Non-Andean members	169·0	77·1	72,191·6	81·8	427
LAFTA	219·2	100·0	88,308·7	100·0	403

Note: GDP figures have been converted into dollars using the free
exchange rates, wherever applicable.
Source: Computed from data provided in IMF, International Financial
Statistics, XXII, 5 (1969)

very uneven fashion, as seen from Table 14. The degree of
industrialization (ratio of gross value-added in industry to total
output) also varies considerably—from 10·8 per cent in Bolivia
to 33·2 per cent in Argentina.[19]

Intra-regional trade is modest, and the Association has not
given it the fantastic boost experienced in the case of the CACM.

[19] INTAL, La integración económica de América Latina, Buenos Aires, 1968, 12.

G

In 1954, a time when Latin American trade was strongly governed by bilateral agreements, intra-zonal exports amounted to 10·3 per cent of total exports. In 1967, after six years of multilateral tariff reductions, intra-zonal exports had declined to 8·2 per cent of total exports. It represents, however, a very modest rise from a share of 6·2 per cent in 1961, when the Treaty entered into force. It should be added that 80 per cent of the intra-regional trade is represented by Argentina, Brazil, Chile, and Peru. Although their relative share is small, Colombia's trade with LAFTA has tripled and that of Mexico has quadrupled. Raw materials and intermediate products for use in industry represent about 60 per cent of the intra-regional imports; consumer goods and foodstuffs represent only 16 per cent.

There is no set policy on the entry of other countries into the Association The latest members are Venezuela (1966) and Bolivia (1967) and their entry has given rise to unexpected procedural difficulties. The attitude at the headquarters is to shy away from problems of a similar nature. CARIFTA appears to be welcome as a unit. In addition to Venezuela and Colombia, who would like to expand their trade into the Caribbean, Brazil and Argentina have also shown interest in CARIFTA's membership. This obviously does not mean that they will agree to it if it ever comes up. The unofficial attitude is the acceptance of granting existing members special arrangements with non-members. This appears to be possible because of LAFTA being a free trade area. Such arrangements, however, should not harm LAFTA and should take into consideration and not clash with regional industrialization agreements which call for common external tariffs.

2. OBJECTIVES

The primary objective of the Treaty is the establishment of a free trade area; eventually a Latin American common market is to be formed. It is expected that the widening of the national markets through trade liberalization will induce accelerated economic development. Although there has so far been only small and tentative progress towards trade liberalization, later institutional developments have at least introduced the acceptance of a policy of industrialization, be it at an embryonic stage; and the incapacity to realize the premises of the Treaty has led to the formation of a subregional group, a common market, with provisions for a comprehensive industrialization and development strategy as shall be taken up later. This subgroup, the Andean Community, has just been formed, hence no implements are yet available for the execution of the policy objectives.

3. POLICY INSTRUMENTS
Since LAFTA is a free trade area, its main instruments lie in the sphere of commercial policy; recent developments point to a sketchy industrialization policy as well.

(a) *Commercial policy*
The contracting parties of the Montevideo Treaty undertake to eliminate gradually all import barriers on commodities originating in other members (Art. 3); to extend to other members the most-favoured-nation treatment (Art. 18); to abstain from subsidizing exports (Art. 52); and to abstain from increasing import duties for products that have been liberalized (Art. 48). There are the usual safeguard clauses against damages to vital sectors of the economies (Art. 23), especially agriculture (Art. 28), and limited preferential treatment for the relatively less-developed members (Ecuador and Paraguay) giving them transitory advantages not applicable to other members and allowing them to follow a less taxing liberalization programme (Art. 32).

Elimination of import restrictions are agreed upon product by product after prolonged and cumbersome multilateral negotiations which give rise to the preparation and amendment of two lists of commodities; the national list and the common list.

The national list differs from country to country and contains the concessions recognized by each member to others. The only requirement is that the reduction in the weighted average of the regional tariffs on commodities included in the national list should be at the annual rate of 8 per cent of the weighted average of tho tariffs on the same commodities imported from the rest of the world. So far there have been only seven negotiations.

The common list contains all the commodities, restrictions on the intra-zonal imports of which are to be totally eliminated by 1973. This list applies to all members. Four negotiations are to take place by then, considering in sequence commodities that represent 25, 50, 75, and 100 per cent of the reciprocal trade.

There is also a third list which specifies the commodities subject to unilateral concessions recognized to the relatively less-developed members.

The following figures are indicative of the little use made by members of recognized concession. In 1965 the national list included 8,470 commodities; only 2,900 of these were actually in intra-regional imports, which means that LAFTA effectively used only 34 per cent of the negotiated concessions. By the end of 1967 there were 10,382 items in the national lists. [20] Considering that in the past years intra-regional trade has been stagnant, the free trade area must have made effective use of even a smaller proportion of negotiated concessions. This is also indicative of the fact that so far negotiations have been made on concessions that do not predominantly enter intra-regional trade.

(b) *Industrialization policy*
LAFTA does not have a comprehensive industrialization policy. Each member continues to follow a policy of import substitution and industrial promotion on a national scale. It would have been unrealistic, in a free trade agreement and under Latin American conditions of import substitution, that members abstain from establishing an industry because another member would be more suitable from the point of view of its location, just as much as to expect that national industries would be sacrificed for the ideal of intra-regional competition.

What LAFTA does provide is 'complementation agreements' (Arts 15–17). [21] These agreements provide for a programme of

[20] *Boletín de la Integración*, IV:41 (1969), 164.
[21] See also Resolución 99, *Cuarto período de Sesiones Ordinarias*.

trade liberalization for products of specific industrial sectors negotiated between two or more members; other members are free to join later on. It is expected that thereby efforts will be made to promote and co-ordinate the national industrialization policies in given sectors. Initially the products of these sectors were to be included automatically in the national lists. But, since reciprocity is a basic premise of the Montevideo Treaty and the member who included the product of a complementation agreement into its national list did not necessarily receive reciprocal concessions from all other members, only a few complementation agreements were signed at the beginning. Subsequently this regulation was repealed and replaced by a clause which states that the benefits derived from such agreements can be passed on to non-contracting members by means of a reciprocal treatment obtained from them. Up to date there are eight complementation agreements in effect in the fields of electrical and electronic equipment, chemical and petrochemical products, and glass. [22]

A relatively new Resolution[23] brings LAFTA to a new stage of development. It recognizes that the objective of the Montevideo Treaty is to promote a balanced economic and social growth of the members by progressive integration of their economies, assigns special importance to the integration of economic sectors, and calls for the establishment of regional industries. The first three fields selected are basic metals, petrochemicals, and paper and cellulose. Exhaustive studies are to be made on existing and prospective capacity, existing and potential demand for their products, use of inputs, and prices. The interesting features of this programme are that for the first time it calls for a common external tariff on products of industries selected to be of region-wide bearing, talks of a jointly programmed strategy for the location of industries to be able to distribute

[22] Statistical machines (Argentina, Brazil, Chile, Uruguay); electronic valves (Argentina, Brazil, Chile, Mexico, Uruguay); household electrical equipment (Brazil, Uruguay); electronic equipment (Brazil, Uruguay); certain chemical products (Colombia, Chile, Mexico, Peru, Uruguay, Venezuela); certain pharmaceutical products (Bolivia, Colombia, Chile, Peru); household goods (Argentina, Uruguay); glass (Argentina, Mexico).

[23] Resolución 100, *Cuarto período de Sesiones Ordinarias*.

equitably the benefits of integration, and brings in a concept of policy harmonization in that it allows for incentives in the country of location and prevents the other members from undermining such incentives.

But 'Resolución 100' is a mere broad policy outline. It does not provide for action measures, and so far no specific action has been taken for its implementation. No agreement has been reached on the types and extent of the required incentives, on the criteria by which to determine the location of industries, etc. There was hope at LAFTA headquarters in the beginning of this year that the instrumentalization of the industrialization policy might start some time in 1970.

Moreover, LAFTA suffers from the lack of institutions which would be of assistance in devising technical measures. In the CACM the ICAITI (Instituto Centro-americano de Investigación y Tecnología Industrial), one of its oldest institutions, provides technical expertise in every relevant aspect of the industrialization process. The comparable LAFTA institution is the Comisión Asesora del Comité Ejecutivo; but it is no more than a political organism.

IV The Andean Community

1. CREATION AND MEMBERSHIP

The conspicuous differences in the levels of economic development between the LAFTA members have caused concern, especially among those of smaller size, over the inequitable distribution of integration-induced industrialization under the present arrangements provided by the Montevideo Treaty. As the 'common list' is expanded and the liberalization of traditional commodities, which were in any case imported from the member countries, gradually comes to an end, tariff negotiations also become more difficult since one now moves into the sphere of sacrosanct, highly-protected domestic manufactured products. The smaller members of LAFTA are discontented with LAFTA's being more advantageous to the larger ones. Integration to them is meaningless unless it gives them a larger share in intra-zonal trade and promotes growth on an equitable basis by careful choice of industrial sites; otherwise they are bound to become peripheral areas of the larger members.

With this in mind five members of LAFTA—Bolivia, Chile, Colombia, Ecuador, and Peru—have agreed to form a subregional common market within LAFTA somewhat on the lines of the Central American experience, creating a unit comparable in geographical size with Argentina, Brazil, and Mexico. The group, which initially also included Venezuela, was conceived with the Declaration of Bogotá in 1966, with Bolivia joining in 1967. The final agreement was signed in Bogotá on May 26, 1969, and was approved by the Permanent Executive Committee on LAFTA on July 9, 1969.

The five Andean countries had in 1967 a population of almost 50 million, representing 23 per cent of the total population of the eleven LAFTA members, and about 5 million more than the population of Mexico alone. The gross domestic product of the subregion is about one-fifth of that of LAFTA, which is evidence for the concern over the equitable distribution of integration-induced industrialization. The subregion itself is far from homogeneous. In Chile and Colombia import substitution has advanced more and succeeded in reducing the ratio of imports to GDP, while Peru continues to be an open economy. Bolivia and Ecuador are the least developed members of the group with per capita incomes of $194 and $220 respectively and with a small manufacturing sector.

The group, having just been formed, is naturally not keen on entering into negotiations with new entities until all its organisms and instruments are well established. If the Community were to look for new members at all, it would be looking for economies with similar characteristics to their own,[24] rather than get involved in the microeconomies of the Caribbean. The philosophy underlying the formation of the Community is import substitution, and hence it is not interested in peripheral primary-product exporting economies, when it is trying to get out of a similar situation itself. Most important is the fact that no

[24] For an interesting proposal on an extended common market combining the Andean group, except Bolivia and Chile, with the CACM, see Rodrigo Botero, *La Comunidad económica Caribe-Andina*, Bogota: Ediciones Tercer Mundo, 1967.

outsider can join the Andean Community without becoming first a member of LAFTA; or LAFTA has to sign a waiver that new members cannot have favourable treatment from the Community alone. There appears to be interest in expanding relations with the Caribbean through increased communications via new maritime lines, and through joint ventures if such ventures could lead to sales in large markets like the EEC. In the Bogotá meeting of mid-1968 a proposal was made to study the economic relations with the Caribbean; however, only Venezuela and Colombia supported the proposal because of their greater trade traffic with the area. The matter is further complicated by existing preferential agreements between the Caribbean countries and their metropoles, by the recent upsurgence of CARIFTA, and by the internal problems from which LAFTA suffers and which make it defer the solution of problematic issues to the future without taking practical steps. The unofficial opinion seems to be that an association on similar lines as that established by the Yaoundé Convention for the associated states and territories of the EEC could be a feasible solution; but the whole development being very new, it is very difficult to make a definite statement.

2. OBJECTIVES

The objectives of the Subregional Integration Agreement[25] are given in Articles 1, 2, and 25. Accordingly, the purpose of the subregional common market is in general to promote the balanced economic development of its members, accelerate their rate of growth, facilitate their participation in the Montevideo Treaty, create the conditions favourable to the transformation of LAFTA into a common market, and to improve the living standards of the people. The benefits of integration must be distributed equitably among the members. Specifically, the objectives are to: (a) accelerate the rate of economic growth; (b) create permanent employment; (c) improve the members' balances of payments; (d) develop infrastructure;

[25] For the full text of the Agreement see ALALC, *Síntesis Mensual*, No. 49, July 1969, 283–316.

and (e) reduce the differences in the levels of development between the members.

3. POLICY INSTRUMENTS

The integration objectives are to be implemented by a number of instruments, some of which are embedded in trade liberalization, and others in the coordination of industrialization and agricultural policies. The main financial institution is the Andean Development Corporation which will provide long-term credit. It should be noted that none of the provisions of the Agreement are yet being implemented, since the Agreement will enter into force when three members have approved it.

(a) *Commercial policy*

Commercial policy instruments of the Agreement consist of a gradual reduction of barriers to intra-Andean trade and the creation of common external tariff. Trade barriers are, in principle, to be eliminated by December 31, 1980, with the exception of those commodities which fall into the scope of complementation agreements or of sectoral development plans which will specify the date of trade liberalization for the product concerned. In general all articles which are in the 'common list' of LAFTA are to be liberalized within six months. Free trade will be applicable to all articles not produced within the region only after the preparation of a flexible list which determines the new products which the region can be capable of producing. Thus, in contrast with the cumbersome product-by-product approach of LAFTA, the Andean Community's tariff reductions are more or less across the board. Agricultural commodities are handled, as usual, in a less liberal fashion.

The common external tariff too will hopefully be introduced by December 31, 1980. This will be in two stages. A minimum common external tariff is to be initiated by December 31, 1970. The final and definitive common tariffs will be applied by 1980. The rates of the common tariff will vary according to existing developmental policies and will be determined according to the incidence of the duties, relations between rates on finished and unfinished products, productive capacity of the area, relative prices (domestic vs. external), and will take into consideration the effects on balance of payments and public revenues.

In both instances, i.e. removal of trade barriers and establishment of the common external tariff, Bolivia and Ecuador, the two least developed members of the subregion, are accorded special treatment through a less taxing schedule and longer period (up to 1985) of trade liberalization (see Chapter XIII, Sections C and D of the Agreement).

(b) *Industrialization policy*
Similar to the model provided by the CACM, the major pillar of the industrialization policy is the joint planning of industrial activities in order to provide for a specialized industrial production, to make full use of available resources, to improve productivity, and to take advantage of economies of scale. The industrialization plans will be coordinated by sectors and will have to specify the sector, investments called for, location of the plants, the required harmonized incentive and trade liberalization policies, and the common external tariff. Industries established or expanded under such programmes will have access to the entire market of the subregion. The Andean Development Corporation will play a major role in this aspect of integration, since it will provide the large portion of funds necessary for pre-investment surveys as well as the actual carrying out of the projects.

V. The European Economic Community

Our main interest is not in the EEC as such but in the relations that some of our selected less-developed countries can possibly have or already have with the Community. This is all the more relevant considering the United Kingdom's past and renewed attempts to become its seventh member and the preferential economic ties that Trinidad and Tobago, Barbados, and Jamaica already have with Great Britain. In the following, therefore, the focus is on the relation between the EEC and its associated states, and on its policy towards less-developed areas.

On March 25, 1957, Germany, France, Italy, Belgium, Netherlands, and Luxembourg signed the Treaty of Rome to create a European Economic Community with the aim of establishing what is now known as the Common Market. They pledged that within the timetable provided in the Treaty they would eliminate the customs duties and quantitative restrictions to importation and exportation of goods; that they would establish a common customs tariff and a common commercial policy; that they would abolish all obstacles to the free movement of factors of production; that they would have a common agricultural and transport policy, etc. The Treaty also put forward three additional provisions, one of which is of extreme importance to our topic, that is the Association of Overseas Countries and Territories with a view to increasing trade and pursuing a joint effort towards economic and social development. This provision stems from the fact that four out of six signatories had colonies in the recent past with which they continue to have close economic and social relationships in spite of the legal and constitutional changes that had taken place in the meantime.[26] It is embedded in Part IV of the Treaty.

Accordingly, the reduction in tariffs and quantitative restrictions between the EEC members are to be applied to imports from the associated countries, without the associated countries necessarily being required to reciprocate the preferential treatment extended by the EEC; on the contrary they may be allowed to protect their infant industries and even in some cases to maintain duties for revenue purposes.

The associated countries are required to extend to the entire Community the same privileged trade regulations that exist between them and the specific member state so that there will be no discrimination between the products of member states in

[26] France had a preferential trade policy with her ex-colonies and territories under which she guaranteed them a market for their products often at prices higher than free market prices. Similarly Holland, Belgium, and Italy had, to various extents, sought to provide mutual benefits to their sphere of influence through special trade arrangements, agreements, and financial assistance. With the possible entry of the United Kingdom into the Common Market the same argument would hold for the British areas of the Caribbean.

the associated countries. Member countries are asked to contribute to the financing of investment projects which are essential
to the economic development of the Association. Nationals
and enterprises of the EEC members will be gradually granted
the right of establishment concurrently with the institution of
free establishment within the EEC. In short, Part IV of the Treaty
has three major provisions: a free trade area between the
associated countries and the EEC (but not between the associated
countries themselves); the gradual recognition of free establishment to all nationals and enterprises of EEC members; and the
European Development Fund (EDF) to provide funds to finance
infrastructure projects, pre-investment studies to explore
industrial possibilities, and vocational training schemes and
scholarships to improve and/or create the required supervisory
and administrative personnel.

An implementing convention was annexed to the Treaty
giving the particulars and the procedure concerning the association conceived in Part IV. But in order to take account of the
political independence of the associated territories acquired
since, and to meet the challenge coming from the East to these
countries[27] by stimulating and maintaining economic development through aid, it became essential to renew the convention
which was to expire at the end of 1962. Hence the Yaoundé
Conference.[28] The provisions of the Yaoundé Convention
became effective approximately seven years after the signing of
the Rome Treaty; they were valid for five years, and members
were free to withdraw from the Convention unilaterally. The
basic provisions were:[29]

(a) The EEC maintains the right to decide in the last resort
the level of its external common tariff, its common trade and

[27] EEC, Commission, *Relations between the African States and Madagascar
and the EEC.* Address by Henri Rochereau to the Symposium on Africa, The
Hague, October 29, 1962; 4–5.

[28] The Convention was signed in Yaoundé on July 20, 1963, and entered into
force on June 1, 1964. For details see 'Les Accords d'Association Successifs avec
les Etats Africains et Malgache Associés et leur Fonctionnement', *Chronique de
Politique Etrangère,* XIX,5, September 1966.

[29] *Ibid.* and EEC, La Convention de Yaoundé, *L'Association des Pays et Terri-
toires d'Outre-Mer à la C.E.E.,* Brussels, 1965–8, 150*/LLL/1965/5.

agricultural policy, and the associated states maintain the right to take trade policy decisions, including the right to withdraw from the membership in the association.

(b) The associated states are free to form customs unions and/ or free trade areas among themselves, provided of course that these agreements are not incompatible with the provisions of the Convention.

(c) The Convention does not bar the entry of other developing countries with similar economic structures who are not signatories to the Convention. [30]

(d) The EEC members are to reduce their tariffs and import quotas on products originating from the associated states at the same rate as they reduce them among themselves. The tariff reduction by the Six is to take place immediately. The associated states are to reduce their import duties at an annual rate of 15 per cent and to eliminate import quotas within four years.

(e) Should economic and fiscal conditions require it, the associated states can, upon consultation with the EEC, maintain or increase import duties or quotas, and introduce new ones in order to protect their infant industries and/or prevent budgetary imbalances. Similarly, the EEC members are also permitted to take measures to safeguard their external financial stability, to prevent serious economic disturbances in one or more of the members.

(f) In order to promote economic development and to safeguard industrialization and to stabilize prices of traitional products at a reasonably remunerative level, the EEC agrees to offer supplementary assistance to the associated states in providing funds, through the EDF, to reinforce economic and social infrastructure, to finance directly productive industrial and agricultural activities and to give technical assistance. They are also entitled to receive financial assistance to mitigate the undesirable effects of temporary fluctuations resulting from abrupt changes in world market conditions.

[30] For instance, an association agreement was signed with Nigeria on July 16, 1966.

The EEC has two institutions for the provision of financial resources for development: the European Investment Bank (EIB) and the EDF. The former is a bank for the Common Market as such, although lately it has been interested in projects in the associate states, such as the development of bauxite resources in Western Surinam. The latter is specifically for the less-developed associate members of the EEC.

The general policy of the EIB is to devote a large part of its resources to projects in less developed regions of the EEC members favouring fairly large-scale projects. The Bank's philosophy is that the initiative for creating new industries can, in practice, come only from fairly large concerns or groups of concerns. It prefers to deal with a small number of large projects rather than with a large number of small ones. In this respect the Bank is less well adapted to meet the need to establish smaller-scale secondary industries.

The main purpose of the EDF is to prepare the industrial development of the underdeveloped associates, by providing the basic facilities, and refraining from direct investments in industry proper. Although it has not refrained from financing tea and palm plantations in various parts of Africa, the direct execution by the Fund of industrial projects is the exception rather than the rule. The reason is that a profitable investment project should, by definition, be self-paying, and hence should be financed out of loans and not grants, so that its profitability can be appraised properly. Yet, by the rules and regulations of its establishment the EDF was allowed only a policy of grants, which has barred it from financing schemes, or parts of schemes, which were profitable. In later years it has been agreed that the Fund may make loans on normal terms for productive schemes of a normally profitable nature. This stems from the acceptance of the need to industrialize as the real solution to the problem of economic diversification.

The Yaoundé agreement ran out at the end of May 1969, and was renewed on June 28, 1969. It will enter into force after ratification by the contracting parties and notification of its conclusion by the European Community. It will have a duration of five years but will expire no later than January 31, 1975.

The structure and the general concept of the new convention have remained largely the same. While continuing to favour the development of trade between the EEC and the associated states, the new convention now also takes into account the encouragement of the development of intra-regional trade and co-operation—through the formation of customs unions, free trade areas, and economic co-operation agreements—and of general preferences in favour of less-developed countries which has emerged during the New Delhi Conference of UNCTAD in 1968. It stresses increased economic independence of the associated states through the promotion of, especially, industrial production. The common external tariffs of the EEC for a number of tropical products are lowered; general aid to production in the form of price support has been abandoned in favour of *ad hoc* intervention commodity by commodity, should falling world prices seriously jeopardize the economy of an associated country. The less-developed signatories of the Convention continue to benefit from the provision which allows them to impose import duties and/or quantitative import restrictions to protect their own industries and/or to meet budgetary deficits. The amount of financial and technical assistance out of the EDF as well as the EIB are increased, with more emphasis on industrial promotion.

The integration schemes discussed in this chapter are the possibilities open to the Caribbean countries with which we are concerned. Theoretically not closed to any country which is willing to meet the conditions and regulations stipulated by these schemes, any of them may constitute a choice. In fact, the three English-speaking countries of our selection of five are full-fledged members of CARIFTA, and Surinam is an associate member of the EEC. It remains to be seen whether or not these arrangements will be permanent, whether and which economic grouping the Dominican Republic will enter (as we have seen it has applied to CARIFTA), and whether CARIFTA as a bloc, or any member of it individually, could associate with the other three integration blocs. While Chapter 6 of Part III discusses the static and dynamic effects of alternative associations devoid from any socio-political considerations, it is nevertheless necessary to survey, be it briefly, the historical and political credibility and viability of the possible alternatives. This will be the subject-matter of Chapter 5 of the following Part.

Part III

APPLICATION OF THE THEORY TO CARIBBEAN COUNTRIES

H

Chapter 5

CHOICE OF ALTERNATIVE
INTEGRATION PATTERNS FOR
THE SELECTED COUNTRIES

The subsequent chapter will assess the consequences of the integration of the five selected countries with some of the existing integration movements briefly described in the previous one. Our methodology ideally calls for evaluating five alternatives for each of the five countries: each country under study could join one of the four integration groups or remain unattached. Twenty-five cases, therefore, present themselves. This would make the analysis rather tedious and repetitious. The economic reality of the region, however, comes to our aid in such a situation, since all countries, except one, have already made economic arrangements with some existing trade bloc. To recapitulate, Jamaica, Barbados, and Trinidad are members of CARIFTA as well as being the driving force behind its formation: Surinam is an associate member of EEC; and the only country outside of any formal integration arrangement is the Dominican Republic.

A question may be raised as to why alternative integration possibilities need be studied, since only one of the five countries has the 'freedom' of choice, so to speak. The answer is that the economic advantages and disadvantages of joining economic blocs can only be evaluated if each country's present position is contrasted with at least one alternative. Such a comparison between the 'present' and 'implied' situation may lead to suggestions as to what co-ordinated action may have to be taken by the individual countries. For instance, it might be feasible for Jamaica to make arrangements with CACM while continuing to be a member of CARIFTA. Conversely, the

115

conclusion might be reached that the 'present' situation is the optimum as far as the Jamaican economy is concerned.

What is proposed here is a selection of limited alternatives, as opposed to five, for each country as follows:

(i) Jamaica:
continue to be a CARIFTA member
join CACM
become associate member of EEC

(ii) The Dominican Republic:
join CACM
join CARIFTA

(iii) Surinam:
continue to be an associate member of EEC
join CARIFTA
join LAFTA

(iv) Trinidad and Tobago:
continue to be a CARIFTA member
join LAFTA
join CACM
become associate member of EEC

(v) Barbados
continue to be a CARIFTA member
become associate member of EEC

The above scheme provides a minimum of two alternatives for each country. Although in each case, except for the existing arrangements, the alternative is hypothetical, its choice is not haphazard. It is in fact a selection taking into consideration not only strict trade relations, but a host of non-economic factors, such as historical and social continuity and existing political relations. For instance, were we to depend solely on the consideration of trade relations, then there would be but one alternative: some sort of association or integration with the US market, since in terms of both exports and imports the United States plays a predominant role in the Caribbean. Given the political set-up in the Caribbean, however, under no circumstances can this be considered as an alternative. Rather, it will have to be treated within the formation of the general policy of the advanced economies, arising from UNCTAD II, to grant tariff concessions to the products of less-developed countries.[1] Moreover, selection of alternatives based solely on trade patterns is not only counter to the essence of our theory of integration for less-developed countries, with its stress on industrialization, but assumes the continuation of the current economic situation which the countries are trying to change. The current economic relations may have the advantage of access to a large market and large amounts of capital inflows; but they also perpetuate, to a large extent, the existing economic structure with reliance on the production of a few major traditional products.[2]

The basis for reasonable and/or acceptable alternatives will have to be sought elsewhere. In the case of the Commonwealth Caribbean countries, CARIFTA needs no justification; likewise for Surinam and the EEC. This is the *de facto* situation which we will evaluate. However, the rationale behind the selection of EEC as an alternative for Jamaica, Trinidad and Tobago, and Barbados, has to be explained. Similarly an explanation is required of LAFTA's trading partnership with Surinam and Trinidad and Tobago, CACM's with Jamaica, Trinidad and Tobago, and the Dominican Republic, and CARIFTA's again with the Dominican Republic.

Prima facie many of the countries have hardly any trade relations with some of the blocs. For instance, the Dominican Republic imports negligible amounts from CACM and has no exports to the area. Jamaica also has no economic contact with this Central American bloc. The same can be said for the

---

[1] The United States has outspokenly reiterated that even if the other developed countries were not to go along, it would take action to consider such concessions to the Latin American countries, among which presumably is the Caribbean. (See the speech of President Richard Nixon on November 10, 1969.)

[2] For the case of the French Antilles and their complete dependence on France and EEC and the detrimental economic effects of such dependency, see Fuat M. Andic, 'The Development Impact of the EEC on the French and Dutch Caribbean', *Journal of Common Market Studies*, VII:1, September 1969, 19–49.

relations between Surinam and LAFTA. Although Barbados imports from the EEC, its exports there are insignificant.

Yet, these economic blocs make sense as alternatives. A ministerial mission from CARIFTA contacted Brussels in October 1969 for the purpose of seeking new arrangements for exports, especially in the event that the United Kingdom joins the European Common Market. Therefore, for CARIFTA members associate membership in the EEC could become a reality although at some high-levels of political echelons doubts are expressed as to its feasibility. In the eventuality that the United Kingdom does become a member of the EEC, the likelihood of which is now stronger than ever, the three Caribbean countries in question, due to their preferential trade arrangements, may force the United Kingdom to demand for them a relationship similar to the one between the EEC and the ex-French colonies in Africa and ex-Dutch colonies in the Caribbean. Our hypothetical scheme of considering EEC as an integration alternative for Jamaica, Barbados, and Trinidad and Tobago (in fact with and without UK participation in the EEC) is based on these premises, in addition to economic factors relating to size.

The choice of LAFTA for Surinam and Trinidad and Tobago departs from the premise that both countries consider themselves South American. Trinidad and Tobago is already a member of the Organization of American States (OAS), and of the Inter-American Development Bank (IDB). It played host to the first meeting in October 1968 of the Co-ordinating Commission of LAFTA and CACM. The meeting discussed, among other things, the possibility of convergence of LAFTA and CACM taking into consideration the interest of non-member countries and of trade and industrial agreements with such countries. [3] We should add that the headquarters of the Caribbean Office of the Economic Commission for Latin America

[3] Comisión Coordinadora ALALC–MCCA, *Informe de la primera reunión de la Comisión Coordinadora ALALC–MCCA* (Port-of-Spain, Trinidad and Tobago, October 14–18, 1968). In this meeting Trinidad and Tobago was represented by eight persons, Jamaica had two observers, and CARIFTA was represented by its Secretary General, again as observer. The meeting also resolved that non-LAFTA/OAS members should attend the subsequent meetings of the Co-ordinating Commission.

is located in Port-of-Spain. Although never openly stated, both in Surinam and in Trinidad and Tobago one can sense a *rapprochement* towards Latin America, which may or may not materialize. Surinam, moreover, does not find the EEC association particularly to its economic advantage. Whatever economic and financial advantage it has derived so far from Western Europe originates basically and substantially from its political association with Holland alone.[4] LAFTA is also a more meaningful alternative for Trinidad and Tobago and Surinam if one recollects that the Andean Community within LAFTA, especially Colombia and Venezuela (the latter has yet to decide whether or not it will join the Community), are specifically interested in extending their market to the Caribbean. Obviously these are interests expressed by the alternative itself, but the country for which the alternative is suggested looks positively upon such interrelations to extend its own market into the area.

CARIFTA is being considered as an alternative for the Dominican Republic and Surinam; it represents a strong reality. Although the Dominican Republic has no trade relations with this economic bloc, and those of Surinam are not overpowering, CARIFTA, as a functioning regional integration bloc, has been making strong overtures to non-CARIFTA members in the region. In fact, at the fifth meeting of the CARIFTA Council in January 1970 there was a warm response to the proposal by Trinidad and Tobago to extend the membership of CARIFTA to the Dominican Republic, Haiti, and the Bahamas. Such an extension would expand the market by about 8·5 million people and add approximately $17 million to the subscribed capital of the Regional Development Bank. The Dominican Republic itself has officially expressed its desire, albeit in general terms, in co-operating with an economic bloc by signing the Declaration of Presidents of Punta del Este in April 1967, and consequently has looked into the possibility of co-operation with both CACM and LAFTA prior to its very recent application to

---

[4] See F. Andic, *op. cit.* However, the continuation of the association with EEC cannot be discarded as a possibility, since recently EEC has shown effective interest in feasible economic projects in Surinam. The association being a fact, it will not be discussed here.

CARIFTA. It is, therefore, not surprising that its government has finally sought membership in it. Undoubtedly the addition of such a relatively large market and productive potential would lend strength to CARIFTA by expanding its size, as well as contributing to a healthy degree of competition with manufacturers of other members.

Finally, CACM has been selected as an alternative for the Dominican Republic and Jamaica. The former country had expressed serious interest in joining CACM, and actually requested INTAL to evaluate alternative possibilities of integration, among them CACM.[5]

The CACM alternative for Jamaica is based on a somewhat different foundation. As far as the authors are aware, there has been no negotiation between the two parties in establishing special economic relations of the integration type. Jamaica's possible co-operation with CACM is basically for the sake of argument, so that we can evaluate the integration possibility of a country like Jamaica with an economic bloc composed of countries with similar economic structures. At the moment trade between the two is practically non-existent.

The previous arguments are partly conjectural; they are based upon personal impressions, interviews, press releases and so on, and they represent an attempt to explain why at least some of the alternatives are perhaps more likely than others. No prophecy is attempted as to what course each country will actually follow. Even if the individual courses of action were to be known, there still remains the attitude of the economic blocs toward the individual countries with which they are, in some cases hypothetically, associated. For instance, CACM and LAFTA might be reluctant, in the short run, to enlarge their membership, because at the moment the former is faced with grave internal problems caused by a brief war between two members and the latter's 'less-developed' members would be

[5] Ramón Tamames, *Las alternativas de la República Dominicana frente a la integración económica de América Latina*, Buenos Aires: Instituto de Integración de America Latina [INTAL], 1967. The report in fact looks descriptively at those alternatives—Caribbean, CACM, and LAFTA—and reaches the conclusion that the Dominican Republic should apply for full membership in LAFTA while seeking preferential agreements with CACM.

reluctant to see their newly acquired privileged status extended to new members. Even the differences in language might constitute a barrier. On the other hand, all indications are that LAFTA is interested in the long run in expanding its activities to the entire South American continent by including Surinam and Trinidad and Tobago, and by possibly uniting with CACM. EEC may not be averse to strengthening its foothold in the Caribbean or to making a concession to the United Kingdom to allow her Commonwealth partners to become, say, associate states. In this connection, the possibility also should be mentioned that the present African associate members might oppose an arrangement of this nature.

This might be the appropriate point at which to evaluate briefly in a non-quantitative manner, as opposed to the quantitative analysis of the subsequent chapter, the likely advantages and disadvantages of the various alternatives for each country.

The EEC offers, under the stipulations of the Yaoundé Convention (see Chapter 4, Section V), technical assistance, financial assistance from the European Investment Bank but especially from the European Development Fund, and a vast fund of technological know-how which could be accessible to the less-developed country through its association with the economically advanced community.

Various remarks can be made on these points. First of all, the practice indicates that the impact of the Caribbean's regionally limited association with the EEC has not been very encouraging. It is somewhat difficult to draw general conclusions with respect to the entire Caribbean from the experience of the French Antilles and the Dutch Caribbean. Even the experience of these two areas of the region does not lend itself to a fully applicable general conclusion. This is due partly to factors relating to economic structure and partly to differences in policies of France and Holland *vis-à-vis* their ex-colonies. One can, however, contend that so far the argument of economies of scale brought about by extended markets has found no substantiation in the Caribbean, since the products of the area have continued to be sold in the protected markets of their respective metropolitan countries, without reaching those of the remaining EEC members whose main interest has been to maintain their existing trade relations and institutions. The development assistance funds have not been of considerable benefit. Heavy emphasis has been laid on infrastructure, partially by the fact that the EDF, by definition, was able to help finance only infrastructural projects and carry out preinvestment studies, but has not executed directly any industrialization project.

Secondly, the Caribbean in essence falls within the North American sphere of influence (United States and Canada). Although the exact amount is not known, there is considerable United States and Canadian investment in the region, not to mention Dutch capital invested in Surinam and loans by international agencies. For instance, in the Dominican Republic US economic assistance has been substantial. But apart from this, IDB has authorized $14·2 million between 1964 and 1967 basically for infrastructural development and is expected to provide another $36 million for various projects of a similar nature. The World Bank is aiding in the setting up of a private nickel exploitation project which could involve a total investment of $180 million. In Jamaica, US economic assistance has been increasing, the World Bank has made considerable commitments and large amounts of private investment have been attracted, especially into the fields of bauxite, alumina and tourism. Trinidad and Tobago receives sizeable multilateral funds for infrastructural purposes and because of the preponderance of oil in its economy has succeeded in attracting substantial foreign (US) private investment. In addition, in most of the countries there is technical assistance provided by the Agency for International Development as well as its Canadian counterpart.

Thirdly, one of the stipulations of the EEC is that for products of less-developed associate members to enter duty-free into the Common Market the source of the firm's investment must consist largely of capital provided by EEC members. Hence future industrialization, if any, can come only through EEC funds, and private capital imports from the United States and Canada may have to be cut down, unless a compromise solution is found the applicability of which would have to extend also to the already existing non-EEC capital.

Fourthly, it should be mentioned that the size of the Caribbean economies being so small, the establishment of new industries also requires that the private foreign investor provide the market of his product. In other words, the market is determined by the foreign investor and that product is produced for which the foreign investor provides the external market. Historically, this has generally been the United States. Examples can be found in textiles, bauxite, and alumina in Jamaica; bauxite, alumina and aluminium in Surinam; bauxite and nickel in the Dominican Republic, tourism in all of the five countries; and oil in Trinidad and Tobago. Consequently, although there is truth in the statement that technological know-how can be transferred from the developed to the less-developed country by the latter's association with the former, only that technology would be introduced, which would be brought in by a specific investor in a specific field.

Fifthly, it is quite likely that the association of a less-developed country with a developed one may create obstacles to its industrialization and import substitution efforts by merely forcing it to remain within its traditional export structure, since it may prove impossible for the less-developed country to compete with the developed one in any line of activity even if transportation costs were assumed to be zero. The association would not enable the less-developed country to protect its industry by high tariff walls.

A final point that comes to mind is the disadvantage of joining an already formed integration bloc with already negotiated and accepted common external tariffs and other norms regulating the economic institutions. Granted, such norms and regulations can be transformed to suit the purposes of the new association; nonetheless such changes and alterations would require considerably greater political dexterity and effort than would the entry into an integration bloc which is being formed and the economic regulations of which are currently being decided upon.

In the meta-economic sphere one 'psychological' advantage

of CARIFTA is that it is formed of countries with similar economic structures facing similar problems. The individual country identifies itself with ease with the general problems of the region, since it itself has undergone the same experience: unemployment of like nature and size, incapability of diversification of products, limitations of size etc. Moreover CARIFTA is still in its initial stages of development; its scope and form are being determined gradually day by day. Member countries therefore have the case of negotiation and creating the form most suitable for them as opposed to the entry of a firmly established and codified bloc.

On the other hand, in CARIFTA member countries may find themselves in positions of conflicting interest. At least in the short run, similarities of economic structure, competition in intra- and extra-Caribbean Trade, the limited size of the market, the desire for rapid industrialization through import substitution, and the absence of common industrialization policies may create thorny problems, as evidenced by the initial experience of CACM.

CACM in certain respects might be a desirable alternative as opposed to CARIFTA or LAFTA, in that its industrialization policy provides for a distribution of feasible industries among the member countries. As was discussed in Chapter 4 the new members should benefit from the scheme of integration industries, which also provides clauses conducive to monopolistic conditions for the newly established industries. Moreover, CACM has the institutional facilities through which it offers the government of the member countries, as well as private investors, technological services. For instance, ICAITI (Instituto Centroamericano de Investigación y Tecnología Industrial) is active in the field of economic and technological research, renders consulting services to private and public sector alike, acts as a bureau of standards, and, on request, prepares marketing and feasibility studies. The existence of such facilities may not necessarily constitute a permanent relative advantage, since undoubtedly similar institutional arrangements will also be made in due course of time within the framework of CARIFTA. Nevertheless a union with CACM could give immediate access to such institutions instead of waiting for their establishment in CARIFTA proper.

In addition to ICAITI, CACM also has a regional development bank—CABEI (Central American Bank for Economic Integration)—which provides financial development assistance, especially in infrastructure. Currently this does not appear to be a determinant factor, since CARIFTA has succeeded in establishing its own regional development bank. Though at the moment its resources are less than those of CABEI, there is no reason why they should not expand concomitant to the successful developments in CARIFTA, and with the implications of IDB in the area and its role in LAFTA. In fact with CABEI in Central America, RDB in the Caribbean and the involvement of IDB in both, EEC's relative advantage as a fund provider through EDF and EIB should be receding. The major economic advantage of EEC for the area would then be the access to its tremendous market, provided that it is willing to allow the products of less-developed associates to encroach upon it and provided that it is willing to assist them diversify and industrialize.

On the negative side, none of the five countries has any trade relations today with CACM. This assumes that obstacles to establishing markets will be overcome, maritime lines would be opened up for the transportation of the products between members, and also that CACM would resolve once and for all whether it would accept new members.

Our final considerations relate to LAFTA. One apparent advantage is the presence of IDB with its vast resources for industrialization and provision of technical know-how. Obviously it is far more powerful and capable than CABEI and RDB and will be so in the foreseeable future. Moreover, the fact that LAFTA is a free trade area with aspirations towards a common market may provide greater opportunity to new members to assert their positions and be able to shape the future Latin American market according to their likings. However, the very same problem of competing with relatively developed countries, as in EEC, also arises in this case. Common industrialization policy of LAFTA not being formulated as yet may appear to be an advantage for the newcomers, in that they need not be put straight away into a straitjacket, so to speak, and they would be free to industrialize in the direction of their own choice. In reality small and non-industrialized countries, such as our selections in this book, will face a great degree of competition coming from, say, Colombia, Argentina, and Brazil. One could venture to say that the Andean Community might offer a preferable alternative, especially if the special clauses relating to the relatively less-developed members can be extended to the Caribbean.

The pros and cons discussed above are far from exhaustive in allowing complete freedom of decision to make one single choice. Even if they were, they could not be easily quantified, nor weights be attached to them. In the final analysis the decision-maker will have to take them into consideration together with the quantitative aspects, as discussed in the subsequent chapter, to define a course of action for his country. Unless the multifaced complexity of the problem is understood, an analysis of the dynamics of integration would fall short of its aim.

Chapter 6

ANALYSIS OF ALTERNATIVE
INTEGRATION PATTERNS

Chapters 1 and 2 dealt with the theory of a customs union, involving developing countries, and sketched in the statistical methods of evaluating such a union according to the extended theory. It was found that these methods involved extensions or additions to those required for a conventional analysis of the gains or losses according to current customs union theory.[1]

When we come to try to realize in practice the statistical side of the suggested extended theory, it will be appreciated that the data problems are very serious. We are faced with the unfortunate situation that we need *more* data to evaluate a customs union between developing countries whilst *less* are usually available in such countries. Indeed, it is more difficult to implement even the standard theory for a group of less-developed compared with industrialized countries.

We have devoted considerable effort to the conventional statistical analysis, both for an estimation of conventional trade effects, and as a necessary basis for any possible statistical analysis of the extended theory. Accordingly, this chapter has been divided into two major sections: firstly, estimation of trade effects of alternative customs union patterns by standard methods; secondly, estimation of other effects to balance against the trade effects in the extended cost–benefit evaluation.

[1] Typical methods for North American and West European countries can be seen in Balassa and Associates, *Trade Liberalization Among Industrial Countries*, Baltimore: Johns Hopkins Press, 1967.

I. Trade Effects of Alternative Integration Patterns

The general procedure can best be illustrated at the outset by considering the broad treatment of any one of the countries in our survey. As an example let us take Jamaica, at present trading with the major alternative blocs listed. Obviously a re-orientation of trade would occur if tariffs between Jamaica and the blocs were re-arranged. In order to measure the quantitative effects of the re-orientation of trade, it is required that exports and imports be disaggregated not only by blocs of countries, but also by principal commodities. The expansion of exports will

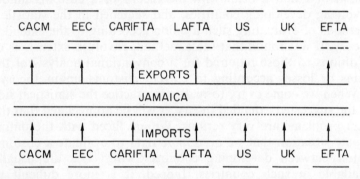

depend on import-price elasticities of demand of foreign countries, and we shall simply take these from statistics for those foreign countries where they are usually only available in a form for aggregate imports (or if disaggregated, not corresponding to Jamaican imports vs. imports from other countries). But for imports we are going to make our own estimations of import elasticities of demand, principal product by principal product, for commodities coming into the Caribbean countries.

In the illustration for Jamaica, above, hatched lines indicate trade flows for which elasticity of demand estimates are required.

As outlined in Chapter 2, three classes of data are required for the calculation of changes in trade: basic import and export patterns, estimates of elasticities of demand, and current and hypothetical future tariff arrangements. Alternative trade patterns can then be derived. We can now enter into detail on these aspects in the following four subsections.

1. BASIC IMPORT AND EXPORT PATTERNS
(a) *Import patterns*

The flow of imports between the countries in our study is shown in Chapter 3. As it stands, the classification there is not in a form completely suitable for the calculation of import price elasticities. For some of those categories, import price elasticities could not be calculated, for others the elasticity estimate is made for a narrower group than appears in the Chapter 3 classification.

Generally, the basis for the import price elasticity estimates are 3-digit SITC categories[2] and these are derived from and combined with base period figures of imports in corresponding form. Three-digit categories will in some cases conform fairly well with homogeneous products meaningfully described by a single demand equation, but not in all cases.

Obviously only a small proportion of 3-digit categories can be dealt with. But in the case of a less-developed country, this is all that is necessary. In a developed country practically all 3-digit categories, at least through the manufacturing categories, would be involved. In a less-developed country, however, significant coverage of imports can be obtained by ten to twelve 3-digit categories.

However, in order to make the elasticity estimates product by product in each country, we cannot proceed directly to the ten to twelve homogeneous products covering the largest slice of imports. For we must take into account the form of the available data. The process adopted was to select all 3-digit categories appearing with any significance in a country's import returns (perhaps 20 or so). These products were then evaluated for data availability, along the following lines:

[2] This was strictly adhered to in the cases of Barbados, Jamaica and Trinidad and Tobago; for Surinam the corresponding 6-digit Brussels nomenclature categories were chosen; in the case of the Dominican Republic, where no international classification was adhered to at the time of the study, the corresponding categories were decided upon examination of the data.

I

(1)	(2)	(3)	(4)	(5)	(6)	(7)	(8)
Principal Products	M_Q	M_V	$P_M = \dfrac{M_V}{M_Q}$	Home price index	Monthly data	Quarterly data	Annual data

1	Are the data available and, if so, for what period?
(by SITC categories) · · · · · · · ·	
20	

where M_Q = quantity of imports, M_V = value of imports, and P_M = unit price of imports.

We filled out this 'availability' table for the 20 or so principal imported products for each of the five countries. Only where we obtained 'yes' through columns (2) to (5), and had a reasonable run of monthly or quarterly data, or a long run of annual data, were we able to estimate the elasticity. Only where we had the data to estimate the desired elasticity measures, did we include one of the 3-digit commodities in the basic import data.

The result of modifying the Chapter 3 classification because of the statistical problems of making elasticity estimates determined the list of major imports studied for each country in Table 15. The list matches up with the availability of elasticity estimates, ready for a calculation of trade changes in sub-section I.4 of this chapter.

The table also takes the opportunity to classify the import duty by source, in line with the various hypothetical integration patterns which have been discussed in Chapter 5. Thus the way is paved for the calculation of trade changes implied by the hypothetical groupings.

(b) *Export patterns*

When we come to exports, we have to rely on the import elasticities of the recipient nations for the exports of the countries in our study. But these elasticities are only available to us¹ in broad terms: as elasticities of classes of imports into blocks of recipient countries.

The information we have on these elasticities is stated in the next section. In a similar way to imports, the exports table (Table 16) presents export data in a slightly modified classification compared with Chapter 3 and also classified by the hypothetical alternatives of Chapter 5. Again, the figures are brought into a form so that, combined with elasticity and tariff data, the trade effects of the various groupings can be calculated in section I.4 of this chapter.

There is some asymmetry in our treatment of imports and exports as indicated at the beginning of Section I. It arises from the fact that imports can be reclassified and studied on the basis of selected significant SITC categories, but there would be little point in a similar treatment for exports unless a further dis-aggregation by country of destination is made for each selected SITC category *and* this could be associated with an import elasticity in each of the markets for which exports were destined. This is a much greater statistical task even than that attempted in this volume for imports.

But there is a more interesting justification for our greater degree of detailed attention to imports compared with exports. The extended theory of customs unions that we have developed has its application to imports. Exports are 'good' for a less-developed country *per se*. Imports, it will be recalled, must be judged by several criteria, such as using foreign exchange, and holding back home industrialization. Thus, in so far as we can apply the extended theory later, it will mainly be to the import side of the trade account.

2 ELASTICITIES OF DEMAND

The calculation of price elasticities of demand in international trade entails problems so far not yet solved. These problems

³ H. Neisser and F. Modigliani, *National Incomes and International Trade*, Urbana: University of Illinois Press, 1953. J. J. Polak, *An International Economic System*, Chicago: University of Chicago Press, 1953. A. C. Harberger, 'Some Evidence on the International Price Mechanism', *Journal of Political Economy*, November 1957, pp. 506–21.

refer to the expected size of the elasticities[3] as well as to the appropriateness of the usually applied method of estimation.[4]

Of the two, the appropriateness of the method of estimation has been questioned and criticized extensively as using 'independent' variables which are not exogenously determined. However, in most small less-developed countries, which do not hold a dominant position in international trade either as suppliers or customers, the method seems to have overcome the objections by the mere fact that their smallness leaves unaffected the exogenously determined world price of the goods concerned. Hence the suitability of the ordinary least-squares method for the calculation of price elasticities seems to have been settled for the countries under study.[5]

In addition, many of the statistical difficulties and unacceptable results which occur in this field of applied work arise from the limited number of observations provided by use of annual data. Recently, this problem has been more and more overcome as quarterly data have become available, so that good results have been obtained even with the commonly applied ordinary least squares method.[6]

The replacement of annual totals by quarterly observations may also solve the problem of normalcy of the time period studied. A shorter time period is more likely to exclude significant structural changes and therefore provide a more appropriate time period for studying demand elasticities.

(a) *Import Elasticities*

For the estimation of price elasticities for the areas studied the following form of demand equation was used:

$$M = a + bp + b_2 Y + b_3 Q_1 + b_4 Q_2 + b_5 Q_3 + u$$

where M denotes quantity of imports, P the corresponding import prices, Y the income of the importing country and Q_i

[4] G. H. Orcutt, 'Measurement of Price Elasticities in International Trade', *Review of Economics and Statistics*, May 1950, 117–32. S. J. Prais, 'Econometric Research in International Trade', *Kyklos*, 15, 1962. L. R. Klein, R. J. Ball, *et al.*, *An Econometric Model of the U.K.*, Oxford, 1961, Ch. 4.

[5] L. R. Klein, 'Single Equation vs. Equation System Methods of Estimation in Econometrics', *Econometrica*, October 1960.

[6] R. J. Ball and K. Marwah, 'The US Demand for Imports, 1948–1958', *Review of Economics and Statistics*, November 1962.

the quarter period (where $i = 0, 1, 2$, or 3). The effect of other variables (time trend, foreign reserves, etc.) not included in the equation must also be examined.

The influence of factors other than price, income, and seasonal variation was considered independently of these variables and is included in the random variable u. The Durbin–Watson 'd' statistic was used as a test of the independence among the residuals. In some cases, the price and/or income variable were lagged for a better fit. These lags, however, were not extended to more than three quarters, which seems a reasonable range.

The coefficients were estimated by application of single equation least-squares, where the explanatory variables were all exogenous so that the estimates have the required statistical properties. Price elasticities were calculated at the point of sample means, i.e.

$$\bar{e}_p = \frac{dq}{dp} \cdot \frac{\bar{p}}{\bar{q}}$$

where $\bar{p}$ is the mean of prices and $\bar{q}$ is the mean of quantities.

Because of the unavailability of independent import price indices, we constructed our own import price index using quarterly value and quantity data for the 3-digit SITC categories. In doing so we encountered several difficulties, one of them being the differences frequently observed in the data between the annual totals and the sum of the quarters. The implications of these observational errors will be discussed later.

In order to facilitate our calculations, the quantity and price data were expressed in index form. To account for the effect of relative prices on imports, import prices should be deflated by an index of the importing country's price level. Although the wholesale price index is most appropriate, the retail price index was used instead of a deflator because other statistics of the price level were not available for the areas studied.

Due to the unavailability of quarterly data for income and the lack of an appropriate procedure for converting yearly data to quarterly data for a developing country,[7] the alternative of using a proxy for which quarterly data are available was

[7] J. H. Lisman and J. Sandee, 'Derivation of Quarterly Figures from Annual

introduced as a substitute for income. The proximity between the yearly data for income and the proxy was detected by calculation of the coefficient of determination. If the proximity between yearly data for income and its proxy was established, it was further necessary to assume that the quarterly movements of the proxy accurately represented movements of income.

In order to account for the short-term fluctuations which accompany quarterly data, instead of adjusting the series of observations we introduced dummy variables into the demand equations. This procedure has the advantage of clearly specifying the degrees of freedom which are used for the accounting of the seasonal influence[8] and is also necessary in view of the shortness of the time series available for some of the areas studied.

Final choice of the best equation among the available alternatives was based on statistical and economic criteria. Statistical criteria include the size of the coefficient of determination and the sizes of the standard errors. Economic criteria include theoretical considerations and *a priori* expectations of the magnitude of coefficients.

The estimates for the areas studied are as follows:

TRINIDAD AND TOBAGO

The following 3-digit SITC categories of imports were studied:

022—Milk and cream
042—Rice
046—Wheat flour
653—Textile fabrics of standard type, other than cotton
681—Iron and steel, including alloy steel
699—Manufactures of metals
721—Electric machinery and apparatus
732—Road motor vehicles

Quantity and total value data are available monthly in the publication *Overseas Trade of Trinidad Tobago*. The study was

Data', *Applied Statistics*, 1964. C. G. Boot, W. Feiber, and J. H. G. Lisman, 'Further Methods of Derivation of Quarterly Figures from Annual Data', *Applied Statistics*, 1967.

[8] L. R. Klein, *An Introduction to Econometrics*, New York: Prentice-Hall Inc., 1962, 35. E. Malinvaud, *Statistical Methods of Econometrics*, Chicago: Rand McNally, 1966, 399.

confined to the period 1960–67 for which 29 observations of quantity and unit price of imports were derived from the monthly data. The unit price indices were deflated by the retail price index. Since quarterly figures for national income are not available, the money supply[9] was used as a proxy. The proximity between income and money supply as measured by the coefficient of determination between the annual observation was $R^2 = 0.923$.

It seems that population changes (emigration) were significant during the period under consideration. However, since these changes are not adequately recorded, we were unable to include a variable for population in the equations.

A variable for the specification of the time trend was introduced and tested, and in some cases it gave significant results.

Except for imports of SITC 721 (electric machinery and appliances), for which a satisfactory price elasticity was not found ($\bar{e}_p = -0.07$), all other imports tested gave price elasticities of demand of the expected sign and size as follows:

SITC	Price elasticity	Income elasticity
022	−0·64	—
042	−0·77	0·67
046	−0·70	1·88
653	−1.44*	1·16
681	−1·58*	—
699	−1·62*	—
732	−1·71*	1.36

* Statistically significant at the 5 per cent level.

The elasticities for foodstuffs (022, 042, 046) were found to be less than unity, as expected. These were also statistically non-significant. Inconsistencies between annual observations and monthly totals, i.e. errors of observation, may account for this non-significance.

In some cases the income variable was found non-significant by the usual statistical tests. For instance, manufactures of metals (699) gave the following equation:

[9] Money supply equals money and quasi-money. IMF, 'International Financial Statistics: Trinidad and Tobago, 1968'.

$$M_t = 114 \cdot 182 - 0 \cdot 342 \, P_t + 0 \cdot 183 \, Y_{t-2}$$
$$ (0 \cdot 004) \quad (0 \cdot 511)$$

$$R^2 = 0 \cdot 755 \qquad d = 1 \cdot 613 \qquad \bar{e}_p = -1 \cdot 54$$

Change in the lag structure and introduction of a time variable T improved the equation but gave a negative coefficient for income, as follows:

$$M_t = 334 \cdot 272 - 0 \cdot 360 \, P_t - 2 \cdot 018 \, Y_t + 2 \cdot 085 \, T$$
$$ (0 \cdot 042) \quad (0 \cdot 842) \quad (0 \cdot 932)$$

$$R^2 = 0 \cdot 814 \qquad d = 2 \cdot 050 \qquad \bar{e}_p = -1 \cdot 62$$

As regards the elasticity for cars (732), the estimation must be accepted with some reservations in view of quantitative restrictions on imports in this area as well as the nature of the good itself.

Some of the results (the low elasticity of electrical machinery and apparatus, negative coefficients of the income variable, non-significant coefficients of foodstuffs) which cannot be explained otherwise, possibly occur through errors of observation and the exclusion of a population variable.

An additional example of a derived demand equation showing significant results was that for textiles:

$$M_t = 121 \cdot 846 - 0 \cdot 704 \, P_t + 0 \cdot 728 \, Y_t - 27 \cdot 868 \, Q_1$$
$$ (0 \cdot 082) \quad (0 \cdot 459) \quad (4 \cdot 361)$$
$$- 23 \cdot 250 \, Q_2 - 20 \cdot 720 \, Q_3 - 0 \cdot 644 \, T$$
$$(4 \cdot 650) \quad\quad (4 \cdot 448) \quad\quad (0 \cdot 444)$$

$$R^2 = 0 \cdot 870 \qquad d = 1 \cdot 845 \qquad \bar{e}_p = 1 \cdot 438$$

BARBADOS

The following 3-digit SITC categories of imports were studied:

012/013—Meat and meat preparations
022   —Milk and cream
042   —Rice
046   —Wheat flour
242/243—Wood, shaped or simply worked
699   —Manufactures of metals
652   —Cotton fabrics
653   —Textile fabrics other than cotton
681   —Iron and steel

Quarterly observations for quantity and total value were obtained from the monthly publication *Overseas Trade of Barbados* for the years 1958–66, giving 35 observations of quantity and unit price. Deflation of the unit prices was made by the retail price index. Money supply[10] was used as a proxy for national income, the coefficient of determination for annual observations between money supply and national income being $R^2 = 0.826$.

Problems relating to the significance of the coefficients of the variables were encountered with regard to foodstuffs. For example, the equation for the imports of milk and cream (022) was as follows:

$$M_t = 18.930 - 0.188\, P_t + 0.998\, Y_t - 38.047\, Q_1$$
$$\quad\quad\quad (0.214)\quad\; (0.190)\quad\quad\; (8.824)$$

$$+ 12.082\, Q_2 + 13.537\, Q_3$$
$$(9.435)\quad\quad (9.319)$$

$$R^2 = 0.643 \qquad d = 2.196 \qquad \bar{e}_p = -0.18$$

and the equation for wheat was:

$$M_t = 126.518 - 0.517\, P_t + 0.312\, Y_t - 11.424\, Q_1$$
$$\quad\quad\quad (0.522)\quad\; (0.125)\quad\quad\; (5.211)$$
$$R^2 = 0.254 \qquad d = 2.700 \qquad \bar{e}_p = -0.52$$

Nevertheless, the calculated elasticities were found to be more or less as expected and are summarized in the following chart:

SITC	Price elasticity	Income elasticity
012/013	−0·13	0·48
022	−0·18	1·03
042	−0·89	0·32
046	−0·52	0·33
242/243	−2·48*	–
699	−0·46	0·58
652	−1·34*	0·32
653	−1·14*	0·83
681	−0·41*	0·87

* Statistically significant at the 5 per cent level.

[10] Money equals money and quasi-money. IMF, 'International Financial Statistics, Barbados, 1968'.

The equations for manufactured goods were among the most interesting. For example, imports of cotton fabrics gave the equation:

$$M_t = 247 \cdot 770 - 1 \cdot 605\, P_t + 0 \cdot 318\, Y_{t-1} - 34 \cdot 935\, Q_1$$
$$(0 \cdot 481) \quad (0 \cdot 250) \qquad (11 \cdot 405)$$
$$- 41 \cdot 259\, Q_2 - 32 \cdot 858\, Q_3$$
$$(12 \cdot 026) \qquad (11 \cdot 008)$$
$$R^2 = 0 \cdot 521 \qquad d = 1 \cdot 501 \qquad \bar{e}_p = -1 \cdot 343$$

And imports of artificial fabrics gave the equation,

$$M_t = 143 \cdot 715 - 0 \cdot 860\, P_t + 0 \cdot 727\, Y_{t-3} - 19 \cdot 925\, Q_1$$
$$(0 \cdot 218) \quad (0 \cdot 343) \qquad (12 \cdot 896)$$
$$- 23 \cdot 163\, Q_2 - 36 \cdot 162\, Q_3$$
$$(12 \cdot 563) \qquad (10 \cdot 686)$$
$$R^2 = 0 \cdot 582 \qquad d = 1 \cdot 209 \qquad \bar{e}_p = -1 \cdot 139$$

THE DOMINICAN REPUBLIC

Imports by the SITC classification have not been available in the Dominican Republic for all the years. Existing statistics for imports were published irregularly for past years and only recently are given in such form. During the period in which this study was conducted unpublished monthly data were obtained through the Central Bank of the Dominican Republic. Quantity and total value data were obtained for all months between July 1965 and June 1968, and quarterly observations were derived from these, yielding 11 observations of quantity and unit price of imports for the following goods:

Refrigerators	Flour
Medicinal compounds	Galvanized steel sheets
Fabrics	Fuel oil
Radios	Gasoline
Codfish	Milk and cream
Road motor vehicles	

Due to the small size of the sample, the number of degrees of freedom was very small, in some cases as low as three, resulting in unreliable statistical estimates.

The unit price indices were deflated by a wholesale price index for Santo Domingo, and money supply was used as an income proxy. All figures were quarterly.

We found elasticities for the following products:

Product	Price elasticity	Income elasticity
Refrigerators	−0·28	—
Radios	−0·93	2·16
Codfish	−0·69	0·75
Milk and cream	−1·26	0·78
Cars	−0·41	4·28

The equation for refrigerators gave a statistically significant price coefficient, but the income variable had a negative sign. This may be explained by the small sample size; in fact, we found the equation for refrigerators as:

$$M_t = 269·038 - 0·264\,P_t - 1·273\,Y - 45·959\,Q_1$$
$$\quad\quad\quad (0·116)\quad (0·318)\quad (4·669)$$
$$-33·931\,Q_2 + 12·36\,Q_3$$
$$(4·582)\quad\quad (6·162)$$

$$R^2 = 0·976 \quad d = 2·202 \quad \bar{e}_p = -0·275$$

This gave a price elasticity of demand for imports of −0·28 which seems very low for refrigerators, a 'luxury' manufactured good. The same may be said for the demand for imports of cars, for which we found the following equation:

$$M_t = -302·687 - 0·395\,P_t + 4·232\,Y_t + 35·755\,Q_1$$
$$\quad\quad\quad (0·436)\quad (0·741)\quad (7·469)$$
$$+30·426\,Q_2 + 33·907\,Q_3 - 4·409\,T$$
$$(7·498)\quad\quad (8·942)\quad (1·530)$$

$$R^2 = 0·954 \quad d = 2·604 \quad \bar{e}_p = -0·412$$

The elasticity for the import demand of milk and cream seems very high in relation to similar products from the other countries studied. Marginal differences among these products may be explained by the different income levels of the areas, and a lower income in the Dominican Republic would justify a slightly higher elasticity for milk and cream. Yet the great difference encountered may only be explained in this case by observational errors in the Dominican Republic data or the very small sample size.

The demand for gasoline was found to be price inelastic as theoretically expected for a necessity without close substitutes. Excluding the price variable, we found the following equation for gasoline:

$$M_t = -452 \cdot 913 + 5 \cdot 388 \ Y + 48 \cdot 937 \ Q_3$$
$$(0 \cdot 495) \quad (6 \cdot 614)$$
$$R^2 = 0 \cdot 955 \quad d = 2 \cdot 706$$

JAMAICA

The following 3-digit SITC categories of imports were studied.

042—Rice
046—Flour
243—Wood, shaped or simply worked
641—Newsprint and other printing paper
651—Cotton yarn and thread
653—Synthetic fabrics
681—Iron and steel
732—Road motor vehicles

Quantity and total value data are available on a monthly basis in the *External Trade Bulletin* published by the Government of Jamaica. Our study covered the period 1959–67 (3rd quarter), for which 34 observations of quantity and unit price of imports were derived from the monthly data. The unit price indices were deflated by the retail price index. With quarterly figures for national income unavailable, money supply (money and quasi-money) was utilized as a proxy for income. The coefficient of correlation for annual observations between money supply and national income for the years 1960–66 is $r = 0 \cdot 89$.

The following elasticities were derived for the various Jamaican imports studied:

SITC	Price elasticity	Income elasticity
042	−1·31*	1·03*
641	−0·82*	1·08*
651	−1·94*	1·08
653	−0·55*	1·38*
681	−0·38*	1·45*
732	−1·12	1·85

* Statistically significant at the 5 per cent level.

For the estimation of the demand for imports of rice, the following equations were calculated introducing income lags for all but the first.

$$M_t = 142{\cdot}067 - 1{\cdot}343\,P + 0{\cdot}849\,Y_t - 23{\cdot}149\,Q_3$$
$$\qquad\quad (0{\cdot}548)\quad (0{\cdot}199)\quad\ (10{\cdot}523)$$
$$R^2 = 0{\cdot}529 \qquad d = 2{\cdot}061 \qquad \bar{e}_p = -1{\cdot}307 \qquad \bar{e}_y = 1{\cdot}034$$

$$M_t = 145{\cdot}947 - 1{\cdot}265\,P + 0{\cdot}771\,Y_{t-1} - 24{\cdot}513\,Q_3$$
$$\qquad\quad (0{\cdot}580)\quad (0{\cdot}208)\quad\ \ (11{\cdot}070)$$
$$R^2 = 0{\cdot}477 \qquad d = 2{\cdot}099 \qquad \bar{e}_p = -1{\cdot}231 \qquad \bar{e}_y = 0{\cdot}940$$

$$M_t = 142{\cdot}331 - 1{\cdot}193\,P + 0{\cdot}761\,Y_{t-2} - 27{\cdot}716\,Q_3$$
$$\qquad\quad (0{\cdot}588)\quad (0{\cdot}210)\quad\ \ (11{\cdot}144)$$
$$R^2 = 0{\cdot}468 \qquad d = 2{\cdot}000 \qquad \bar{e}_p = -1{\cdot}160 \qquad \bar{e}_y = 0{\cdot}928$$

$$M_t = 133{\cdot}553 - 1{\cdot}126\,P + 0{\cdot}807\,Y_{t-3} - 35{\cdot}832\,Q_3$$
$$\qquad\quad (0{\cdot}587)\quad (0{\cdot}219)\quad\ \ (11{\cdot}334)$$
$$R^2 = 0{\cdot}475 \qquad d = 2{\cdot}017 \qquad \bar{e}_p = -1{\cdot}096 \qquad \bar{e}_p = 0{\cdot}984$$

From these four equations, the first was chosen in view of the larger R^2 value and the smaller standard errors. The 1st and 2nd quarters of the year were found non-significant and were eliminated from the equations in order to obtain a better fit.

Good equations were also achieved for the demand for newsprint and other paper. It was found that income lagged by two quarters gives a better equation although the dummy variables for the quarters are statistically non-significant. When the income variable was not lagged, the dummy variables for the quarters became significant but the R^2 was reduced. The two equations with and without lagged income respectively are given below:

$$M_t = 95\cdot612 - 1\cdot233\,P + 1\cdot137\ Y_{t-2} + 13\cdot439\ Q_1$$
$$(0\cdot575)\quad(0\cdot228)\qquad(14\cdot064)$$
$$+9\cdot479\ Q_2 + 15\cdot476\ Q_3$$
$$(14\cdot568)\quad(13\cdot917)$$

$$R^2 = 0\cdot632 \qquad d = 2\cdot232 \qquad \bar{e}_p = 0\cdot816 \qquad \bar{e}_y = 1\cdot081$$

$$M_t = 84\cdot412 - 1\cdot130\,P + 0\cdot992\ Y + 28\cdot767\ Q_1 + 39\cdot274\ Q_2$$
$$(0\cdot554)\quad(0\cdot216)\quad(14\cdot140)\quad(14\cdot397)$$
$$+37\cdot977\ Q_3$$
$$(14\cdot123)$$

$$R^2 = 0\cdot585 \qquad d = 2\cdot037 \qquad \bar{e}_p = 0\cdot772 \qquad \bar{e}_y = 0\cdot935$$

The equations for the demand for cotton yarn were also satisfactory. We found no seasonal variation, and the inclusion of a variable for the time trend gave a better fit. The best equation for cotton yarn, for which the income variable is non-significant, is given below:

$$M_t = 245\cdot258 - 2\cdot128\,P_t + 0\cdot888\ Y_{t-3} - 2\cdot294\ T$$
$$(0\cdot281)\quad(0\cdot645)\qquad(1\cdot588)$$

$$R^2 = 0\cdot714 \qquad d = 2\cdot850 \qquad \bar{e}_p = 1\cdot939 \qquad \bar{e}_y = 1\cdot028$$

The equations derived for synthetic fabrics (653) and iron and steel (681) were satisfactory, but the equation for cars (732) gave non-significant coefficients for price and income.

SURINAM

Imports into Surinam are not classified according to the SITC but may be found in monthly publications of external trade put out by the government (*Maandstatistiek van der in- en uitvoer per goederensoort en per land*). Available data for our study covered the period 1963 (4th quarter) to 1968 (1st quarter), for which 18 observations of quantity and unit price indices were derived from the monthly quantity and total value data given in the sources. The following imports were studied:

Flour	Cotton fabrics
Meat products	Lifting and extracting machinery
Fuel oil	Road motor vehicles
Medicinal compounds	Tractors
Rubber products	Radio equipment
Iron and steel	

The unit price indices were deflated by an index of consumer prices for families in Paramaribo and money supply (money and quasi-money) was used as an income proxy. The correlation coefficient between annual totals for income and money supply for the years 1962 through 1965 was found to be $r = 0.95$.

The following elasticities were found:

Product	Price elasticity	Income elasticity
Flour	−1·77*	2·70*
Meat products	−0·67*	2·29*
Medicinal compounds	−1·61*	0·83
Rubber products	−1·05*	—
Cotton fabrics	−1·85*	1·23
Lifting equipment	−1·62*	1·64
Motor vehicles	−1·22*	2·57*
Radio equipment	−1·08	2·05

* Statistically significant at the 5 per cent level.

The equation for flour has all the variables for seasonal variation and time trend significant, as seen below:

$$M_t = 98.785 - 1.902\,P_t + 1.901\,Y_t + 17.684\,Q_1$$
$$(0.633) \quad (0.803) \quad\quad (9.585)$$

$$+ 24.104\,Q_2 + 48.173\,Q - 4.452\,T$$
$$(8.709) \quad\quad (8.564) \quad (1.788)$$

$$R^2 = 0.593 \qquad d = 1.413 \qquad \bar{e} = -1.769 \qquad \bar{e} = 2.068$$

The equation for oil gave the price variable non-significant as theoretically expected. Eliminating the price variable, the co-efficient of determination of imports of oil with income and time as explanatory variables was $R^2 = 0.945$.

The equation for radio equipment did not give satisfactory

results from a statistical standpoint and the elasticities of income and price are not significant.

In general the elasticities came out as expected with the correct sign and size. Exceptions to this were flour, which gave a rather high price elasticity for a necessary foodstuff, and road motor vehicles, which have a large price elasticity where greater dependence on income might be expected.

In summary, for the five countries studied we examined 47 demand equations for various imports, and we found 35 price elasticities of the theoretically expected sign and magnitude. The number of observations used was adequate in each case, except for Surinam and the Dominican Republic. However, the quality of the data was frequently suspect, often showing inconsistencies between the annual totals and the monthly and/or quarterly figures. We may conclude that observational errors were, at least in some cases, the cause of statistically weak results.

Since some of the countries (Surinam and the Dominican Republic) do not record their foreign trade transactions in the Standard International Trade Classification, and the content of the same (3-digit) SITC number was not always identical for common products chosen for the countries, comparison among the different estimates of similar groups of products chosen for separate countries is not possible. Nevertheless, it seems that consistency has been achieved for some products. For example, textile fabrics (651, 652, 653), which may be assumed to be relatively homogeneous product categories, gave the following elasticities:

Country	Price elasticity
Trinidad and Tobago (1961–68)	−1·44
Barbados (1958–66)	−1·34
Jamaica (1959–67)	−1·94
Surinam (1964–68)	−1·85

Marginal differences may be attributed to different tastes and differing levels of income; further, there is not complete consistency in the periods studied for each country (indicated by brackets above).

In general, the results are satisfactory when measured against the economic and statistical criteria adopted for the study, and better results could be achieved only through more careful reporting of foreign trade statistics by the countries involved.

(b) *Export Elasticities*
By these we mean not export elasticities of the Caribbean countries, but import price elasticities of customers of Caribbean countries. As already stated, estimations by ourselves are not feasible in this case. Estimates do exist for particular products for 'typical developed countries' or for USA (the latter is often taken as representative of the former).[11] Below we list estimates available for the commodities which appear in the export data of the tables, and note in the end column the compromise figure we have utilized in the calculation of trade changes.

Elasticities of Demand for Caribbean Imports by Foreigners

Commodity	Tinbergen[a]	Ball and Marwah[b]	Kreinin[c]	Present study
Sugar	−0·4	−0·36	−0·34	−0·4
Paper		−1·38	−0·39	−1·0
Tobacco		−0·26		−1·0
Cocoa		−0·34	−0·34	−0·4
Coffee	−0·4	−0·34	−0·34	−0·4
Bauxite		−0·26		−0·3
Banana	−0·7	−0·34	−0·34	−0·7
Timber		−0·26		−0·3
Rum		−1·87	−1·29	−1·5
Rice		−0·34	−0·34	−0·4
Lard and margarine		−1·87	−1·29	−1·5
Textiles		−0·38	−0·39	−1·0

Notes: [a] Jan Tinbergen, *Shaping the World Economy*, New York: Twentieth-Century Press, 1962.
[b] R. J. Ball and K. Marwah, *op. cit.*
[c] M. Kreinin, 'The Effects of Tariff Changes on the Prices and Volume of Imports,' *American Economic Review*, LI, June 1961.

[11] As in B. Belassa and Associates, *Trade Liberalization Among Industrial Countries, op. cit.*

K

In using these rounded and common figures for each product for all imports into developed countries we are following common usage, but we are stretching the assumption to include small quantities of exports to fellow CARIFTA countries.

3. TARIFF LEVELS

(a) *Tariffs on Caribbean Imports*
The same list of commodities as for base import quantities and elasticities must obviously be used, and then as near an appropriate tariff expressed (tariff categories may not exactly correspond to these categories).

The tariffs stated are nominal—directly from legal rate schedules—and not effective as recently derived from input–output data,[12] a statistical enterprise normally impossible in less-developed countries. In the case of Commonwealth Caribbean countries, the dual tariff structure of Commonwealth Preference has, of course, to be taken into account.

(b) *Tariffs on Caribbean Exports*
In completing the statistical picture ready for calculating the trade effects of different possible groupings, we require tariffs on the export side matched with base period export values and price elasticities in the customer countries.

Some difficulties present themselves. There is the elasticity of supply in the exporting countries, and demand in the importing countries. No information is available on the former, so we unhappily assume perfect elasticity of supply. On the import countries side, as before, we use nominal or legal tariffs. As in the case of elasticity estimates, work on the basic statistics of imports of customer countries would be extensive and out-of-balance for the study.

Thus, for example, tariffs shown are Commonwealth preference legal rates for the UK imports, the common external tariff for the EEC imports, etc.

For some countries account has to be taken of dual tariff structures according to country of origin of the import. This is clearly the case for the UK. But also the EEC tariff and the

[12] See chapter 2.

CARIFTA tariff must be differentiated accordingly as the trading partner is a fellow member of the customs union (or associated state) or not.

In the case of LAFTA, several differentiations ought to be made as there is a multiple tariff structure according to country of origin. But here we have simplified down to a weighted average for each commodity weighted by import values from the different trading countries.

A straight elasticity exercise in projecting trade changes on the basis of these actual and implied hypothetical tariff changes is not highly accurate. This is because of the quota and other international agreements affecting many of these products. One should interpret the quantitative results of the next section carefully in the light of quota restrictions which would still operate as tariffs changed.

4. CHANGES IN TRADE PATTERNS OF ALTERNATIVE INTEGRATION GROUPINGS

It is only a matter now of applying well-known methods, sketched at the outset of the present section of this chapter, to the base imports, elasticities, and alternative tariff arrangements now all given for both imports and exports of two standard lists of commodities.

This has been done and summary tables of results appear at the end of this chapter.

II. Developmental Effects of Alternative Integration Patterns

We have eliminated from the set of possible alternatives for each of our five Caribbean countries those which have a small degree of political reality. We are now able to state the trade implications, subject to well-known qualifications, of the feasible alternatives, where there *is* some existing trade on which to base projections.

A conventional customs union analysis, such as we have used in Chapter 1, is not appropriate for less-developed countries, and would stop here. The 'best' alternatives ignoring political aspects would now be apparent.

However, following the extended theoretical analysis of Chapters 1 and 2, each integration alternative should now be evaluated from the point of view of the four criteria: foregone national product, the foreign-exchange saving, new capital requirements, and the general benefits of industrialization.

This is a new endeavour, and in view of present data limitations, cannot be carried through completely in this volume. But we can go some way, with a statistical analysis in the case of some of the effects, a qualitative discussion of others, for those alternatives where we have a trade change, so as to emphasize how the non-trade effects must be set against those stemming from trade.

1. FOREGONE NATIONAL PRODUCT THROUGH INCOMPLETE SPECIALIZATION

It will be recalled that the first of the four elements in our evaluation function to judge between integration alternatives is the short-fall of trade and income compared with following unobstructed free trade.

There is some question of what meaning can be attached to the comparison of various 'second-best' trade positions with the free trade optimum. But to keep as closely as possible to the Cooper–Massell theory upon which we built our own, we shall beg this question at present. In any case, we are only using the *differences* between free trade and the trading volume of various alternatives as relative measures.

A more important objection might be that 'free trade' is a meaningless concept institutionally for the countries in question: rather the 'point of comparison' might be the integration alternative offering maximum trade. This might well be used to measure the comparative loss of trade, etc., of the other alternatives. It has one disadvantage. We do not then have any idea of the magnitude of loss involved in all customs unions, actual or hypothetical, compared with pursuing a policy of all-out free trade. It so happens that the differences in loss between alternatives for the Caribbean are very small; is the loss for all of them compared with wider free trade also very small, or very large?

Thus, in spite of the difficulties, we use the unlikely free trade option as a focal point from which to measure relative loss of trade or welfare through partially denying specialization following comparative advantage.

The hypothetical free trade position for each of our five countries is estimated as follows.

The difference between 'free trade' imports and present imports is calculated from:

$$(M_F - M_1) = e \cdot t/1 + t \cdot M_1$$

where M_1 = 'present' imports (1965/66), M_F = 'free trade' imports, e = an average import demand elasticity for all imports, calculated from the elasticities for individual products, $i = 1, 2, \ldots j$, that we ourselves estimated:

$$e = \sum_{i=1}^{j} e_i M_i / \sum_{i=1}^{j} M_i$$

We also employ an average tariff on all imports calculated in a similar way:

$$t = \sum_{i=1}^{j} t_i M_i / \sum_{i=1}^{j} M_i$$

Exports under free trade have been calculated in a slightly simpler way:

$$(X_F - X_1) = e \cdot t/1 + t \cdot X_1$$

where X_F = exports under free trade, X_1 = 'present' exports (1965/66), and where, since we did not ourselves make export price elasticity calculations, a rough average of those we did use has been employed, namely $e = -0.5$ and $t = 0.10$.

The results are as follows (in units of US $000);

Trinidad and Tobago
$$(M_F - M_1) = (-1.35)\,(-0.082)\,\$567,167 = \$51,856$$
$$(X_F - X_1) = (-0.50)\,(-0.091)\,\$435,174 = \$20,018$$

Barbados
$$(M_F - M_1) = (-0.77)\,(-0.098)\,\$69,721 = \$5,229$$
$$(X_F - X_1) = (-0.50)\,(-0.091)\,\$28,570 = \$1,314$$

Dominican Republic

$$(M_F - M_1) = (-1.06)(-0.305) \, \$160,753 = \$51,923$$
$$(X_F - X_1) = (-0.50)(-0.091) \, \$136,716 = \$ \ 6,835$$

Jamaica

$$(M_F - M_1) = (-1.13)(-0.12) \quad \$294,078 = \$39,877$$
$$(X_F - X_1) = (-0.50)(-0.091) \, \$210,120 = \$10,506$$

Surinam

$$(M_F - M_1) = (-1.00)(-0.152) \, \$94,976 \ = \$14,436$$
$$(X_F - X_1) = (-0.50)(-0.091) \, \$57,659 \ = \$ \ 2,652$$

With these hypothetical free trade figures to hand, it is now possible to measure the loss that the actual (the present) and hypothetical alternative groupings imply.

The simplest approach is to use trade straightforwardly as a measure of this loss:

Reduction in Trade Under Alternative Country Groupings (US $000)

		Present ($)	CARIFTA	EEC ($)	EEC and UK ($)
Trinidad and Tobago	M	51,856	51,856	54,002	35,009
	X	20,018	18,872	18,152	16,553
	T	71,874	70,728	63,154	51,562
Barbados	M	5,229	5,229	4,570	2,413
	X	1,314	1,134	1,311	1,296
	T	6,543	6,363	5,881	3,709
Dominican Republic	M	51,923	51,923	43,919	—
	X	6,835	6,830	6,434	—
	T	58,758	58,753	50,353	—
Jamaica	M	39,877	39,877	36,731	31,977
	X	10,506	10,481	10,294	8,964
	T	50,383	50,358	47,025	40,941
Surinam	M	14,436	14,436	11,076	—
	X	2,652	2,599	2,652	—
	T	17,088	17,035	13,728	—

It was apparent from the statement of import and export predictions under alternative groupings other than the present that there was relatively small trade expansion. It can now be seen that the present situation represents a substantial 'loss' of trade compared with free trade. And that the alternative groupings do little to ameliorate this loss. All of the alternatives considered involve a substantial 'loss' on the first criterion of trade foregone.

The results can be translated into welfare measurements (refer to Figures 6 and 8 of Chapter 2), using the commonly accepted formula:[13]

$$\Delta W = \tfrac{1}{2}(t/1 + t)\,(M_i - M_F) \qquad i = 1, 2, 3.$$
$$+ \tfrac{1}{2}(t/1 + t)\,(X_i - X_F)$$

where $(t/1 + t)$ is the relative average height of the tariff under each alternative group compared with zero tariffs under free trade.

The results of these calculations give a loss of welfare for each alternative (the CARIFTA alternative differs so little from the present that it is not shown separately) compared with free trade as follows:

(US $000)

		Present ($)	EEC ($)	EEC and UK ($)
Trinidad and Tobago	M	2,126	1,845	1,435
	X	921	835	761
	T	3,047	2,680	2,196
Barbados	M	256	224	118
	X	60	60	60
	T	316	284	178
Dominican Republic	M	7,944	6,720	—
	X	314	296	—
	T	8,258	7,016	—
Jamaica	M	2,393	2,204	1,919
	X	483	474	412
	T	2,876	2,678	2,331
Surinam	M	1,097	842	—
	X	122	122	—
	T	1,219	964	—

[13] H. G. Johnson, 'The Gains from Freer Trade with Europe: An Estimate', *Manchester School*, September 1958.

The question now arises of evaluating compensating advantages of the present and alternative restricted trade groupings.

2. THE FOREIGN EXCHANGE GAP

Compared with free trade, all of the restricted trade alternatives involve a more substantial cut-back of imports than of exports. Therefore there is a substantial gain on the second criterion for the alternatives (CARIFTA not stated) as measured by $(M_F - M) - (X_F - X)$:

Foreign Exchange Savings Under Alternative Country Groupings (US $000)

	Present	EEC	EEC *and* UK
Trinidad and Tobago	31,838	26,850	18,656
Barbados	3,915	3,259	1,117
Dominican Republic	45,088	37,485	—
Jamaica	29,371	26,437	23,013
Surinam	11,784	8,424	—

This is not a complete account of the foreign exchange position under each alternative. For, as will be argued in a moment, each of the alternative groupings offers different industrialization possibilities, and these will impose new demands for foreign exchange.

3. COSTS OF CAPITAL FOR INDUSTRIALIZATION AND BENEFITS FROM INDUSTRIALIZATION

These third and fourth criteria for choice between the alternative groupings, which we shall consider together, are, of course, the most difficult to evaluate, though some measure of the latter can be approximated by the new (urban) employment created by an industrialization project.

There are two aspects to the problem of capital costs. First, we need hypothetical data of what the fixed and working capital cost would be for the location of particular industries in the region. Secondly, some knowledge would be desirable as to which industries would be set up under the different integration alternatives.

Information is not entirely lacking on the first. Studies of potential industries for the Caribbean and Central America exist, looked at from the point of view of capital cost *and* some of the benefits, particularly employment creation.[14]

This information is valuable, but is along industrial sectoral lines, whilst our orientation is along politico-geographical lines, of alternative groupings of countries which might sign an integration pact. Of course, the two approaches are by no means exclusive; an actual agreement may well cover certain *sectors* for a particular *group* of countries.

It does, however, involve a somewhat different treatment statistically. For example, Brewster and Thomas, in a very interesting table,[15] predict the import saving and capital cost of complete or partial replacement of imports into the West Indian region by home industry, *sector by sector*. We, on the other hand, have studied the total import bill, by alternative politico-geographical grouping.

Whilst we would claim our approach as slightly more interesting, since that of Brewster and Thomas effectively compares the present situation with a no-trade situation in listed sectors, our approach is certainly less convenient statistically because it is difficult to know which industries would be set up in which countries until the political agreement between any of the groupings we have hypothesized is signed.

Certainly, both the Brewster and Thomas and our own approach are complementary in future integration planning. It is a matter of articulating their sectoral analysis for our differing politico-geographical alternatives. Thus, for example, the future iron and steel sector should be evaluated as regards projected imports at some target date, and consequential target domestic capacity, required capital and employment creation, not for the *one* integration policy (as in Brewster and Thomas) but for *each* of those discussed here.

[14] W. Brewster and C. Thomas, *The Dynamics of West Indian Economic Integration*, Institute of Social and Economic Research, University of the West Indies, Kingston, Jamaica, 1967; and UN/ECLA, *Possibilities of Integrated Industrial Development in Central America*, New York, 1964.

[15] Brewster and Thomas, *op. cit.*, p. 283.

With this can be deduced the 'foregone national income' of each alternative along lines discussed earlier, the foreign exchange saving of each, the capital-cost and the employment benefit. This will total over sectors to quite different aggregate benefits/ costs for different alternatives since the agreed sectoral pattern will differ sharply in alternative groupings.

Each politico-geographical alternative is really a different set of potential industrial sectors. The economic evaluation of *each alternative* implies completion of a table such as this:

Country

Sector	Implied loss of national income	Foreign exchange saving	Capital loss	Employment creation
1				
2				
.				
.				
.				
n				

Each alternative implies a different sub-set of sectors 1, 2, ... *n*. The economic benefit of integration is the sum of columns 2 to 5 over the sub-set. Work like that of Brewster and Thomas and our own is necessary for the development plan of a developing country. This important question—of the relation between this integration work and the development plan—is taken up in our concluding remarks.

Conclusion

In concluding this chapter, let us briefly review what we have achieved, and where further progress is indicated.

Sources of data are a serious problem. There must be serious deficiencies in actual collection and reliability of trade statistics on which we are unable to judge. But taking trade statistics as published, two problems might be mentioned. The time-series are short and perhaps not homogeneous; this problem should solve itself in due course. But the SITC, which some developing countries use, is a classification system really geared to developed countries, as is the Brussels system of classification of imports and exports. Thus the peculiar effect arises of the bulk of a country's trade falling under a few 3-digit categories. Instead of being able to work with broad 1- or 2-digit groups, these few sub-items of the complete classification become overwhelmingly important. Following from these observations, it might be best to try to improve the statistical quality of just the 3-digit categories listed in this book.

For the non-trade evaluation, the statistical picture is very deficient. It would appear that, as an adjunct to the formation of the development plan, the capital cost and employment creation of the setting-up of many hypothetical industries should be calculated. This, and the import–export effects through other sectors of the expansion of one industry requires more effort on input–output studies.

These statistical deficiencies noted, we can claim to have extracted the maximum which is possible from the trade statistics in the calculation of elasticities for the countries used as examples. This has led to an estimate of the trade 'loss' of the present trading arrangements, and alternative ones, of considerable interest.

Against these different trade 'losses' must be set the other evaluation criteria of integration possibilities which we have discussed at length in our theoretical chapters. Statistical problems at present prevent a full development on this side to match the work on trade.

This work seems to us an essential part of development plans. It is already done to some extent, at least for some industries, but not from the economic integration viewpoint—the various costs and benefits by industry for different integration possibilities.

To move in this direction would help to bring together the economics of integration and development economics, both of which tend to go along their separate paths at present, a situation which does no service to the formulation of economic policies for developing nations.

Table 15 Select Imports and Tariffs on Those Imports

| Products | JAMAICA | | | | | | DOMINICAN REPUBLIC | | | SURINAM | | | | | |
| | Imports from | | | | Tariffs | | Imports from | | Tariffs | Imports from | | | | Tariffs | |
	CARIFTA	EEC and UK	EEC	CACM	Pref.	Gen.	CARIFTA	CACM	Gen.	CARIFTA and EEC	CARIFTA	LAFTA and EEC	LAFTA	Pref.	Gen.
Rice	37.3	1.5	1.5		0.0327	0.0436			0.220					0.105	0.130
Milk									0.160						
Flour		29.0			0.158	0.2131			0.729	12.2	0.5	11.7		0.132	0.182
Paper		13.7	1.4		0.1417	0.1958			0.560	44.6	1.3	43.3		0.203	0.235
Textiles		25.8	1.4						0.619	17.7	2.4	15.3		0.135	0.160
Iron and steel		69.9	29.9		0.0458	0.1167			0.331	27.0	0.4	26.7	0.1	0.153	0.186
Manufactures of metals	0.2	49.7	9.8		0.131	0.219			0.106	32.7	12.6	20.3	0.2	0.093	0.104
Machinery: mining and construction		35.0	6.9		0.0367	0.0867				38.9	0.3	38.6			
Machinery: electric		49.5	10.8	0.1	0.1423	0.2077			0.440	39.5	0.4	31.9		0.191	0.220
Road motor vehicles		12.1	5.1		0.1722	0.3388			0.601					0.131	0.154
Miscellaneous manufactures		32.5	6.8		0.2279	0.3246									
Meat products										25.7	1.4	25.1	0.8	0.281	0.281
Rubber										30.6	0.5	32.2	2.1	0.141	0.169
Fish									0.129					0.225	0.240

Table 15 (continued)

Products	TRINIDAD AND TOBAGO Imports from					Tariffs		BARBADOS Imports from			Tariffs	
	CARIFTA	LAFTA	CACM	EEC and UK	EEC	Pref.	Gen.	CARIFTA	EEC and UK	EEC	Pref.	Gen.
Rice	93.0			39.9	27.4	0.018	0.0721	98.6	67.7	51.8	0.0	0.017
Milk		0.1		7.5	6.1		0.0233		28.9	28.9	0.0	0.028
Flour			0.1	34.7	5.0	0.0		9.9	39.4	9.1	0.1	0.2
Paper				28.8	6.2	0.1	0.2	0.1	23.2	2.9	0.05	0.1
Textiles				72.9	9.9			0.4	66.9	5.4	0.075	0.1762
Iron and steel		1.8		55.9	12.3			5.8	62.3	7.7	0.1	0.2
Manufactures of metals	0.1	0.3		36.9	5.5	0.0	0.1	0.5	48.5	7.0		
Machinery: mining and construction	0.1	1.0		42.7	9.1	0.075	0.2	0.7	54.3	8.8		
Machinery: electric		0.4		82.6	8.6	0.131	0.272		85.1	10.5	0.0842	0.21
Road motor vehicles				37.8	10.8	0.1632	0.3263		43.3	12.4	0.13	0.28
Miscellaneous manufactures	0.8	0.2						1.3	5.2	2.9	0.0936	0.178
Meat products												
Rubber												
Fish												

Source: As Tables 1–10.

Notes

1. Imports selected by feasibility of making elasticity estimates.

2. Imports shown in relative shares of each integration alternative in the imports of the individual countries.

Table 16 Selected Exports and Tariffs on Those Exports

Products	JAMAICA						DOMINICAN REPUBLIC		SURINAM							
	CARIFTA		EEC *and* UK		EEC		CARIFTA		CARIFTA *and* EEC		CARIFTA		LAFTA *and* EEC		LAFTA	
	Exports	Tariff	Exports	Tariff	Exports	Tariff	Exports	Tariff	Exports	Tariff	Exports	Tariff	Exports	Tariff	Exports	Tariff
Sugar			63.9	0.000					79.6	0.000	16.4	0.218				
Paper									95.8	0.000						
Cocoa									83.0	0.000						
Coffee	0.4	0.223	52.6	0.000	5.7	0.139			0.2	0.000						
Bauxite									100.0	0.000						
Banana			100.0	0.000	4.3	0.200	0.2	0.158	28.8	0.000			0.3	nr	0.1	nr
Timber											10.9	0.125	100.0	0.000		
Rum			29.9	0.000	7.9	0.000					5.4	0.072	17.9			
Rice									90.4	0.000			85.0			
Lard and margarine																
Textiles									31.9	0.000	11.6	0.264	20.4		0.1	nr

Table 16 (continued)

Products	TRINIDAD AND TOBAGO						BARBADOS					
	CARIFTA		EEC *and* UK		EEC		CARIFTA		EEC *and* UK		EEC	
	Exports	Tariff	Exports	Tariff	Exports	Tariff	Exports	Tariff	Exports	Tariff	Exports	Tariff
Sugar	3.3	0.194	73.1	0.000			0.2	0.194	78.7	0.000		
Paper												
Cocoa			56.2	0.000	26.4	0.054						
Coffee												
Bauxite												
Banana												
Timber												
Rum							47.2	0.000	8.2	0.000	1.3	0.000
Rice							100.0	0.146				
Lard and margarine												
Textiles												

Sources As Tables 1–10.

Notes

1. Exports shown in relative shares going to each integration alternative.
2. Tariffs are omitted where exports are very insignificant (marked nr—not relevant); where an integration alternative is a composite one, with imports mostly going to one bloc, the tariff of that bloc is stated.

Table 17 Jamaica Import Patterns following Alternative Integration Plans
(US $000)

Products	Present Imports from								Imports as Associate Member of EEC							
	USA	EEC	CARIFTA	EFTA	LAFTA	UK	Other	Total	USA	EEC	CARIFTA	EFTA	LAFTA	UK	Other	Total
Rice	4,272	106	2,604	—	—	—	2.8	6,986	4,278	106	2,604	—	—	—	2.8	6,986
Flour	2,371	2,774	—	—	—	—	4,410	9,556	2,357	2,872	—	—	—	—	4,383	9,613
Misc. chemicals	3,192	599	—	212	—	1,422	848	6,274	2,540	1,795	—	169	—	1,216	675	6,397
Paper	3,105	100	—	285	—	898	2,200	7,291	2,586	1,288	—	821	—	778	1,833	7,308
Textiles	1,890	—	—	—	—	1,638	3,093	6,622	1,890	—	—	—	—	1,638	3,093	6,622
Iron and steel	2,032	4,401	—	274	—	5,885	2,122	14,716	1,921	5,069	—	259	—	5,703	2,005	4,958
Metal manufacturers	3,264	988	—	—	—	4,034	1,828	10,116	2,337	3,486	—	—	—	3,264	1,309	0,397
Mining and construction	11,216	1,327	—	302	—	5,437	1,353	19,637	10,364	2,406	—	279	—	5,437	1,250	9,738
Electrical	4,082	1,262	—	—	—	4,522	1,820	11,687	3,874	1,628	—	—	—	4,522	1,727	1,751
Vehicles	1,615	1,122	—	—	—	1,551	17,847	22,136	1,122	7,682	—	—	—	1,270	12,403	2,479
TOTAL	37,044	12,684	2,604	1,775	—	25,390	35,527	115,025	33,267	26,336	2,604	1,929	—	23,829	28,685	1 6,252
MARKET SHARE	32.2	11.0	2.3	1.5	—	22.1	30.9		28.6	22.7	2.2	1.2	—	20.5	24.7	

Table 17 (continued)

Products	Imports as Associated Member of Enlarged EEC						
	USA	EEC and UK	CARIFTA	EFTA	LAFTA	Other	Total
Rice	4,272	106	2,604	—	—	2.8	6,986
Flour	2,357	2,872	—	—	—	4,383	9,613
Misc. chemicals	2,540	3,217	—	169	—	675	6,603
Paper	2,586	2,187	—	821	—	1,833	7,428
Textiles	1,387	3,257	—	—	—	2,270	6,915
Iron and Steel	1,921	10,955	—	259	—	2,005	15,141
Metal manufacturers	2,337	7,521	—	—	—	1,309	11,167
Mining and con-struction	10,364	7,844	—	279	—	1,250	19,738
Electrical	3,874	6,150	—	—	—	1,727	11,751
Vehicles	1,122	9,233	—	—	—	12,403	22,760
TOTAL	32,764	53,345	2,604	1,529	—	27,862	118,105
MARKET SHARE	27.7	45.2	2.2	1.3	—	23.6	

Notes
1. Proportion of total import trade covered by this analysis is 39 per cent.
2. Figures based on 1965.

L

Table 18 Dominican Republic. Import patterns following alternative integration plans
(US $000)

Products	Present Imports from						Imports as Associate Member of EEC					
	USA	EEC	EFTA	LAFTA	Others	Total	USA	EEC	EFTA	LAFTA	Others	Total
Paper, etc.	4,332	1,036	560	—	1,206	7,134	3,058	3,128	395	—	856	7,438
Wheat	5,144	—	—	—	—	5,144	5,144	—	—	—	—	5,144
Milk	1,630	3,049	214	—	16	4,909	1,346	3,903	176	—	13	5,439
Electrical	4,658	834	228	—	1,884	7,604	3,330	3,001	163	—	1,347	7,841
Cotton fabrics	2,600	145	—	—	3,249	5,994	972	3,897	—	—	1,215	6,084
Iron and steel	4,301	3,490	966	—	1,980	10,737	3,526	5,422	792	—	1,623	11,365
Motor vehicles	6,614	2,463	2,379	—	2,223	13,679	5,595	4,569	2,012	—	1,880	14,058
Machinery	5,389	1,545	876	—	2,102	9,912	4,192	3,745	681	—	1,635	10,255
Chemicals	5,051	2,237	1,095	425	1,721	10,329	1,894	8,817	410	159	654	11,927
Dried fish	—	133	2,412	—	1,011	3,556	—	413	2,221	—	931	3,566
TOTAL	39,719	14,932	8,730	425	15,392	79,198	29,060	36,899	6,853	159	10,147	83,120
MARKET SHARE	50·2	18·9	11·0	0·5	19·4		35·0	44·4	8·2	0·2	12·2	

Notes
1. Proportion of total import trade covered by this analysis is 49 per cent.
2. Figures based on 1966.

Table 19 Surinam. Import patterns following alternative integration plans
(US $000)

Products	Present Imports from					Imports as Associate Member of EEC				
	USA	EEC	EFTA	Other	Total	USA	EEC	EFTA	Other	Total
Flour	1,288	192	—	159	1,640	1,024	528	—	126	1,680
Meat, etc.	761	299	78	91	1,230	649	480	67	77	1,274
Rubber	697	541	348	213	1,800	592	801	295	181	1,870
Paper	337	1,019	—	998	2,355	284	1,368	—	842	2,496
Textiles	1,194	538	133	1,644	3,511	892	1,407	100	1,228	3,628
Iron and Steel	7,837	3,603	423	1,658	13,522	6,873	5,198	371	1,454	13,897
Electrical Machinery	2,961	2,374	—	809	6,145	2,241	3,803	—	612	6,657
Motor vehicles	2,252	2,510	1,362	330	6,455	1,887	3,500	1,141	277	6,806
TOTAL	17,330	11,079	2,347	5,905	36,662	14,445	17,090	1,976	4,800	38,312
MARKET SHARE	47·3	30·2	6·4	16·1	—	37·7	44·6	5·2	12·5	—

Notes
1. Proportion of total import trade covered by the analysis is 49 per cent.
2. Figures are based on 1965.
3. Surinam is already as associate member of EEC, but the alternative refers to the removal of present import duties on EEC products.

Table 20 Trinidad and Tobago. Import patterns following alternative integration plans
(US $000)

Products	Present Imports from								Imports as Associate Member of EEC							
	USA	EEC	EFTA	CARIFTA	UK	LAFTA	Other	Total	USA	EEC	EFTA	CARIFTA	UK	LAFTA	Other	Total
Milk and cream	—	1,638	364	—	746	—	3,221	5,970	—	2,239	325	—	721	—	2,879	6,161
Rice	—	—	—	5,187	—	—	388	5,575	—	—	—	5,187	—	—	388	5,575
Flour	812	328	—	—	76	—	4,169	5,385	812	328	—	—	76	—	4,169	5,387
Textiles	2,032	411	—	—	1,484	—	2,655	6,585	1,581	1,722	—	—	1,306	198	2,065	6,678
Iron and steel	2,346	1,525	—	—	9,669	268	1,527	15,337	1,731	4,383	—	—	8,298	—	1,127	15,737
Metal manufacture	2,322	1,285	227	—	4,543	—	2,052	10,430	1,583	3,820	155	—	3,879	—	1,399	10,839
Industrial machinery	13,795	1,268	217	—	7,299	293	369	23,243	11,781	3,596	186	—	7,299	250	315	23,429
Electrical machinery	5,596	1,222	147	—	4,516	—	1,975	13,458	5,033	2,090	133	—	4,516	—	1,783	13,577
Road motor vehicles	528	1,447	—	—	12,483	—	2,420	16,880	447	2,124	—	—	12,483	—	2,047	17,103
Paper, etc.	1,755	356	628	—	2,103	—	2,243	7,086	1,625	880	382	—	1,947	—	2,077	7,113
TOTAL	29,187	9,484	1,585	5,187	42,925	562	21,021	109,954	24,615	21,183	1,382	5,187	40,528	449	18,253	111,599
MARKET SHARE	26.6	8.6	1.4	4.7	39.1	0.5	19.1	—	22.1	19.0	1.2	4.6	36.3	0.4	16.4	—

Table 20 (continued)

Products	USA	EEC and UK	EFTA	CARIFTA	LAFTA	Other	Total
		Imports as Associate Member of Enlarged EEC					
Milk and cream	—	2,981	325	—	—	2,879	6,186
Rice	—	—	—	5,187	—	388	5,575
Flour	812	405	—	—	—	4,169	5,387
Textiles	1,581	3,209	—	—	—	2,065	6,856
Iron and steel	1,731	14,053	—	—	198	1,127	17,110
Metal manufacture	1,583	8,363	155	—	—	1,399	11,502
Industrial machinery	11,781	10,896	186	—	250	315	23,427
Electrical machinery	5,053	6,606	133	—	—	1,783	13,577
Road motor vehicles	447	14,608	—	—	—	2,047	17,103
Paper, etc.	1,625	2,983	582	—	—	2,077	7,268
TOTAL	24,615	64,109	1,382	5,187	449	18,253	113,996
MARKET SHARE	21.6	56.2	1.2	4.6	0.4	16.0	—

Notes
1. Proportion of total import trade covered by this analysis is 23 per cent.
2. Figures based on 1966.

Table 21 Barbados. Import patterns following alternative integration plans
(US $000)

Products	Present Imports from								Imports as Associate Member of EEC							
	USA	EEC	CARIFTA	EFTA	LAFTA	UK	Other	Total	USA	EEC	CARIFTA	EFTA	LAFTA	UK	Other	Total
Flour	176	372	—	—	—	—	737	1,286	174	387	—	—	—	—	729	1,291
Meat	994	153	—	274	1,214	124	2,586	5,346	991	169	—	273	1,210	123	2,578	5,347
Rice	—	—	1,351	—	—	—	18	1,369	—	—	1,351	—	—	—	18	1,369
Milk and cream	—	1,026	—	147	—	314	494	1,982	—	1,077	—	143	—	310	481	2,011
Textiles	504	45	—	—	—	313	677	1,540	397	342	—	—	—	277	533	1,550
Iron and steel	90	82	—	—	—	943	417	1,534	84	157	—	—	—	908	388	1,539
Metal manufacturers	475	193	145	—	—	1,377	332	2,523	439	336	134	—	—	1,320	357	2,538
Machinery	906	158	—	—	—	934	253	2,253	773	487	—	—	—	798	216	2,276
Electrical machinery	988	322	—	—	—	1,671	689	3,670	892	678	—	—	—	1,508	622	3,702
Road motor vehicles	103	374	—	—	—	2,653	427	3,558	72	1,056	—	—	—	2,245	298	3,671
Paper etc.	333	147	160	96	—	489	389	1,617	281	386	133	81	—	428	328	1,640
TOTAL	4,573	2,876	1,656	517	1,214	8,821	7,024	26,684	4,106	5,080	1,620	497	1,210	7,921	6,502	26,938
MARKET SHARE	17.2	10.8	6.2	1.9	4.5	33.1	26.3		15.2	15.9	6.0	1.8	4.5	29.4	24.1	

Table 21 (continued)

Products	*Imports as Associate Member of Enlarged* EEC						
	USA	EEC *and* UK	CARIFTA	EFTA	LAFTA	Other	Total
Flour	174	387	—	—	—	729	1,291
Meat	991	293	—	273	1,210	2,578	5,337
Rice	—	—	1,351	—	—	18.6	1,369
Milk and cream	397	1,391	—	143	—	481	2,015
Textiles	84	655	—	—	—	533	1,586
Iron and steel	439	1,101	—	—	—	388	1,574
Metal manufactures	773	1,713	134	—	—	307	2,594
Machinery	892	1,422	—	—	—	216	2,412
Electrical machinery	72	2,349	—	—	—	622	3,864
Road motor vechicles		3,710	—	—	—	298	4,080
Paper, etc.	281	791	135	81	—	328	1,617
TOTAL	4,106	13,817	1,620	497	1,210	6,502	27,734
MARKET SHARE	14.8	49.8	5.8	1.8	4.4	23.4	

Notes

1. Proportion of total import trade covered by this analysis is 38 per cent.
2. Figures based on 1965.

Table 22 Jamaica. Export patterns following alternative integration plans (US $000)

Products	Present Exports to					Exports under enlarged CARIFTA				
	CARIFTA	EEC	UK	Other	Total	CARIFTA	EEC	UK	Other	Total
Sugar	—	—	27,969	15,789	43,758	—	—	27,969	15,789	43,758
Coffee	3	42	344	344	733	3	42	344	344	733
Banana	—	733	16,354	—	17,088	—	733	16,354	—	17,088
Rum	—	347	971	3,096	4,415	—	347	971	3,096	4,415
Other	2,718	2,721	12,040	126,644	144,124	2,843	2,721	12,040	126,644	144,249
TOTAL	2,721	3,844	57,680	145,874	210,120	2,846	3,844	57,680	145,874	210,245

Table 22 (continued)

Products	Exports as Associate Member of EEC					Exports as Associated Member of Enlarged EEC			
	CARIFTA	EEC	UK	Other	Total	CARIFTA	EEC and UK	Other EEC	Total
Sugar	—	—	27,969	15,789	43,758	—	27,969	15,789	43,758
Coffee	3	44	344	344	735	3	430	344	777
Banana	—	818	16,354	—	17,173	—	17,907	—	17,907
Rum	—	347	971	3,096	4,415	—	1,318	3,096	4,415
Other	2,718	2,846	12,040	126,644	144,249	2,718	15,440	126,644	144,803
TOTAL	2,721	4,056	57,680	145,874	210,332	2,721	63,066	145,874	211,662

Notes
1. Figures are based on 1965.
2. For 'other' exports, projections made on the basis of a removal of a 10 per cent tariff and an elasticity of demand in importing countries of 0.5.

Table 23 Dominican Republic. Export patterns following alternative integration plans
(US $000)

Products	Present Exports to:				Exports under Enlarged CARIFTA				Exports as Associate Member of EEC			
	CARIFTA	ECE	Other	Total	CARIFTA	EEC	Other	Total	CARIFTA	EEC	Other	Total
Bauxite	100	—	10,246	10,346	104	—	10,246	10,350	100	—	10,246	10,346
Other	38	8,587	117,745	126,370	39	8,587	117,745	126,371	38	8,982	117,745	126,765
TOTAL	138	8,587	127,991	136,710	143	8,587	127,991	136,721	138	8,982	127,991	137,111

Notes
  1. Figures are based on 1966.
  2. For 'other' exports, projections made on the basis of a removal of a 10 per cent tariff and an elasticity of demand in
     importing countries of 0·5.

Table 24 Surinam. Export patterns following alternative integration plans (us $000)

	Present Exports to				Exports under Enlarged CARIFTA			
	CARIFTA	EEC	*Other*	*Total*	CARIFTA	EEC	*Other*	*Total*
Paper	160	619	200	979	188	619	200	1,008
Cocoa	—	107	8	112	—	107	4	112
Coffee	—	129	26	155	—	129	26	155
Bauxite	—	90	45,848	45,939	—	90	45,848	45,939
Banana	—	572	—	572	—	572	—	572
Timber	338	557	2,216	3,111	349	557	2,216	3,123
Textiles	43	75	253	373	52	75	253	382
Rice	139	2,184	247	2,571	142	2,184	247	2,575
Other	23	1,574	2,245	3,842	23	1,574	2,245	3,843
TOTAL	704	5,910	51,043	57,658	757	5,910	51,043	57,711

Notes
1. Figures are based on 1965.
2. For 'other' exports, projections made on the basis of a removal of a 10 per cent tariff, and an elasticity of demand in importing countries of 0.5.

Table 25 Trinidad and Tobago. Export patterns following alternative integration plans
(US $000)

Present Exports to

	CARIFTA	EEC	UK	Other	Total
Sugar	784	—	17,308	5,591	23,684
Cocoa	—	676	761	1,120	2,558
Other	23,818	40,323	41,745	303,043	408,931
TOTAL	24,603	40,999	59,815	309,756	435,174

Exports under Enlarged CARIFTA

	CARIFTA	EEC	UK	Other	Total
Sugar	835	—	17,308	5,591	23,735
Cocoa	—	676	761	1,120	2,558
Other	24,913	40,323	41,745	303,043	410,026
TOTAL	25,749	40,999	59,815	309,756	436,320

Exports as Associate Member of EEC

	CARIFTA	EEC	UK	Other	Total
Sugar	784	—	17,308	5,591	23,684
Cocoa	—	690	761	1,120	2,572
Other	23,818	42,177	41,745	303,043	410,785
TOTAL	24,603	42,867	59,815	309,756	437,042

Exports as Associate Member of Enlarged EEC

	CARIFTA	EEC and UK	Other	Total
Sugar	784	17,308	5,591	23,684
Cocoa	—	2,127	1,120	3,248
Other	23,818	85,844	303,043	412,706
TOTAL	24,603	105,280	309,756	439,639

Notes
1. Figures are based on 1966.
2. For 'other' exports, projections made on the basis of a removal of a 10 per cent tariff and an elasticity of demand in importing countries of 0.5.

Table 26   Barbados. Export patterns following alternative integration plans

	Present Exports to					Exports under Enlarged CARIFTA					Exports as Associate Member of EEC					Exports as Associated Member of Enlarged EEC and UK			
	CARIFTA	EEC	UK	OTHER	TOTAL	CARIFTA	EEC	UK	OTHER	TOTAL	CARIFTA	EEC	UK	OTHER	TOTAL	CARIFTA	EEC	OTHER	TOTAL
Sugar	41	—	15,649	4,183	19,873	45	—	15,649	4,183	19,877	41	—	15,649	4,183	19,873	41	15,649	4,183	19,873
Rum	769	21	112	726	1,630	769	21	112	726	1,630	769	21	112	726	1,630	769	134	726	1,630
Lard and margarine	579			—	579	690			—	690	579		—		579	579	—		579
Other	1,431	75	330	4,650	6,486	1,496	75	330	4,650	6,552	1,431	78	330	4,650	6,490	1,431	424	4,650	6,505
TOTAL	2,821	96	16,092	9,559	28,570	3,001	96	16,092	9,559	28,750	2,821	100	16,092	9,559	28,573	2,821	16,207	9,559	28,588

Notes
1. Figures are based on 1965.
2. For 'other' exports projections made on the basis of a removal of a 10 per cent tariff, and on elasticity of demand in importing countries of 0.5.

SUBJECT INDEX

NAME INDEX

Ahiram, A., 50n
Allen, R. L., 15
Andic, F. M., 117n, 119n

Balassa, B., 29n, 30n, 127n, 145n
Ball, R. J., 132n, 145
Bhambri, R. S., 15, 16
Boot, C. G., 134n
Botero, Rodrigo, 103
Brewster, W., 153, 154
Brown, A. J., 15

Castillo, Carlos M., 90n
Chenery, H. B., 39n
Cooper, C. A., 15, 16, 17, 18, 19, 20, 22, 23, 26, 32, 33, 35, 39, 41, 148

Dosser, D., 29n

Feiber, W., 134n

Han, S. S., 29n
Harberger, A. G., 131n
Hazelwood, A., 16n
Hitiris, T., 29n

Johnson, H. G., 151n

Kitamura, H., 15, 16, 18
Klein, L. R., 132nn, 134n
Kreinin, M., 145

Linder, S. B., 15, 16, 17, 18, 26, 41
Lipsey, R. G., 14, 15
Lisman, J. H., 133n, 134n

Malinvaud, E., 134n
Marwah, K., 132n, 145
Massell, B. F., 15, 16, 17, 18, 19, 20, 22, 23, 26, 32, 33, 35, 39, 41, 148
Meade, J. E., 14
Meier, G. M., 15
Mikesell, R. F., 15, 16, 18
Modigliani, F., 131n

Neisser, H., 131n
Nixon, President Richard, 117n

Orcutt, G. H., 132n

Polak, J. J., 131n
Prais, S. J., 132n

Rochereau, Henri, 108n

Sandee, J., 133n
Strout, A. M., 39n

Tamames, Ramón, 78n, 79n, 120n
Thomas, C., 153, 154
Tinbergen, J., 145

Urquidi, V. L., 15, 16, 18

Viner, J., 14

Wionczek, Miguel S., 90n